Seeking Faith
Lessons In Grace

William Batchelor Jr.

Dedication

These essays are devoted to my wife Kathy for her steadfast support and shared travel through life, to my children, that they might be encouraged in their own walks, and to my Father in heaven, who waited lovingly and with great patience for his prodigal to return.

William Batchelor Jr.

Foreword

Life is like this, one night you go to sleep as master of the universe and then something unpleasant wakes you up. We are in control and then we are not. Actually we never were. My road to this realization was slow and leisurely. Seeing it as folly was not the greatest challenge. The true problem was the near impossible task of separating myself from pride and embracing God's truth with the same fearful heart that knows all too well the sorry road I have gladly, if not boastfully walked until now. The human mind is a glorious but utterly deceitful gift. On the one hand it enables our moment-by-moment conscious celebration of this life, but on the other it will readily assume an intoxicated subservience to the material pleasures that permeate this world. All the while, the worldly mind thinks nothing of sacrificing long-term good for immediate gratification. My worldly mind was and remains to this day an arrogant, greedy, demanding voice.

Sadly, betrayal is the one fundamental human behavior that is not exclusive to interpersonal relationships. We betray ourselves each and every day without hesitation, often accompanied by the most fantastical rationalizations. In fact, there is probably no better proof that the soul is separate and apart from the mind than self-betrayal. They are two opposite forces constantly trying to instill their way, unconfined in both scope and adaptability, and they have tested honest human resolve ever since the original first betrayal. So, how do good intentions end up badly just as Paul lamented to the Romans, or more importantly, how can bad intentions ever be redeemed for good? My earnest belief is, one moment at a time, lovingly, and in God's word.

"A life of significance is born in the actions of a single moment", those words sum it up perfectly when I consider the critical moments in my life. Probably just like you, I can close my eyes and usher them up like a highlight reel, one astonishing moment after another. But, as with all of us, those moments are irreversibly bound to the lifelong struggle between mind and soul. They are vulnerable to both material as well as spiritual influence. Thankfully, the truth we discover through God's word is that a single, merciful moment exists which is enough to receive the grace that will assure us of an eternity of more.

I once read that ninety-nine percent of the solution to a problem is first recognizing and admitting that there is one. It is also understood that progress or growth must have a baseline from which to start or we become hopelessly mired in relativism. That moment of revelation when mind and soul accept the existence of an absolute truth is just such a beginning, but it is only the beginning. It is only through that spiritual liberation that the journey seeking and embracing God's absolute truth can finally begin.

These essays, or more affectionately, these devotionals that follow are my humble record of the questions, confrontations, exercises and merciful revelations that God's word has led me through in a discipleship that began when I was fifty-five. I don't claim a perspective more unique or illuminating than any other, but if you accept that my intention is to offer one man's humble appraisal of the many transformative moments he experienced on the merciful road to faith, then you will have the perspective from which I wish to begin, and like Barnabus I pray they will encourage and accompany you on your own road in faith.

> *"The sovereign Lord has given me his words of wisdom, so that I know how to comfort the weary. Morning by morning he wakens me and opens my understanding to his will."*
> Isaiah 50:4

In Christ,

Bill Batchelor
December 2014

Table of Contents

Foreword
Chapter 1 - "Reject Passivity"
Chapter 2 - "Take Off The Blinders"
Chapter 3 - "If It's Only Skin Deep"
Chapter 4 - "Second Chance"
Chapter 5 - "Choices"
Chapter 6 - "What Is Truth?"
Chapter 7 - "Lead Courageously"
Chapter 8 - "Why Should I Want Eternal Life?"
Chapter 9 - "Partnering With God"
Chapter 10 - "To Know Is Forever"
Chapter 11 - "What Is Right?"
Chapter 12 - "If I Have Faltered More Or Less"
Chapter 13 - "Don't Count On It"
Chapter 14 - "The Teacher's Dream"
Chapter 15 - "Obedience Is Better Than Sacrifice"
Chapter 16 - "Confidence From Within"
Chapter 17 - "But I Miss My Old Life"
Chapter 18 - "Self Reliance"
Chapter 19 - "Why Must I Suffer?"
Chapter 20 - "A Monument Not Shaped"
Chapter 21 - "What Will Suffice?"
Chapter 22 - "In Thanksgiving"
Chapter 23 - "Don't Be A One Hit Wonder"
Chapter 24 - "I'm Stuck"
Chapter 25 - "Louder Than Words"
Chapter 26 - "Latch On To The Affirmative"
Chapter 27 - "Where Are My Blessings?"
Chapter 28 - "The Greatest Among You"
Chapter 29 - "Freedom In Obedience"
Chapter 30 - "I Never Knew You"

Chapter 1

"Reject Passivity"

"One day as Jesus was walking along the shore of the Sea of Galilee, he saw two brothers, Simon and Andrew, throwing a net into the water, for they fished for a living. Jesus called out to them, 'Come, follow me, and I will show you how to fish for people!' and they left their nets at once and followed him."

Matthew 4:18-20

    A life of significance is born in the actions of a single moment. That statement is so amazing it bears repeating, "A life of significance is born in the actions of a single moment". The first time I heard those words was early one day, driving down the highway, listening to a guy on the radio talking about authenticity. It was a cold November morning, foggy out. It was miserable wintery weather. It was not a fishing day, and definitely not the best to be driving in. Maybe not so different from the day that Simon and Andrew first had their world turned upside down. I heard those words and the more I thought about them the deeper they burrowed in, like they had been trying to be a part of me all along and I'd just never listened.
    It is so true, we live from one moment to the next, and when you think about it carefully, each successive moment is essentially dependent on, framed in and determined by each crucial moment

that precedes it. Moments represent choices. We cannot know what the future holds except that whatever eventually materializes will always exist in the form of a choice. It may not seem like a choice at the time, because things happen in an instant, it's imperceptible really. But we always have a choice and it is those decisions made in microseconds of time that determine not only our present lives, but the range of possible futures that will ensue. Simply stated, then is determined by now. It seems so unfair when you think about it. There is so little time to make such monumental commitments.

Decisions would be simple if we had plenty of time to consider them, or if we weren't always in such a rush, if things weren't piling up so uncontrollably or loaded with such irreversible consequences. But life is not about time-outs, it's about dealing from moment to moment with all the stuff that comes flying at us. So, if we want to succeed, to survive intact from one moment to the next, willing and able to respond to our lives in a meaningful way, what can we do to prepare ourselves, to improve the odds, to start and continue on a winning streak? More to the point, how do we build a life of significance from the actions of a single moment?

Experience shows us that it boils down to how we deal with that single moment, how we identify it, isolate it and confidently act on it. When you consider the speed and the unexpected nature that most significant moments in our lives occur, a strategy of preparation is the only option that makes sense, all our efforts have to reflect that reality. In order to be timely, any significant action should be a reflex, not a reaction. The trained reflex is much more reliable and authentic than a reaction, and it is far less complex. Reflexes are innate, they are born in repetition, they are hard-wired, and they by-pass the brain. Reactions are exactly the opposite, they arise out of circumstances, they are on the fly, they are never the same, and they are often tinged with emotion.

Like every other skill we aspire to excel at, practice makes perfect. If we can reasonably anticipate the choices, which we will face and if we can thoroughly prepare for those conditions ahead of time then our chances of success, when they eventually occur, improve dramatically. Preparing for the choices in life is not unlike a golfer practicing tee shots on the driving range or a basketball player shooting free throws in the driveway, both are training their minds and their bodies to react favorably when the inevitable challenges arrive. They can respond without thinking, reflexively. Their actions are custom designed for the moment.

The Bible teaches us that all scripture is inspired by God and is useful to instruct us in what is true. It seeks to make us realize what is wrong in our lives. It corrects us when we are wrong and teaches us to do what is right. Preparation in the word and through the word is the ultimate training regimen, it is universally applicable and there are no moments, which might arise that training in the word cannot survive and overcome. Christ promises he will go before us, that he will not fail us or abandon us, that he directs the steps of the godly, and that he alone knows the way we should turn.

Boldly putting my faith in the Lord to decide for me takes the worry out of life's moments, it turns my clumsy worldly reactions into agile spiritual reflexes. Actions born in scripture lead to a life of significance because they assure us of a right walk with Christ. They produce moments we are pleased with, moments we will share, and moments we don't mind confessing. They are the moments that influence those around us to better themselves as well. Most important though, they are not accidental or free of thoughtful influence. They are our fruit. They are the moments, which respect the sacrifice that Christ made for all men. Although, they occur one perilous step at a time, always testing the meager progress that seems to come so dearly, with each success comes the knowledge and the confidence that build endurance and hope. A life of significance begins with the act of faith and every moment, which follows, reflects and strengthens that faith. A life of significance begins on a solid foundation and it builds one moment at a time from there.

Just as crucial as the beginning is what follows, how we live out our faith. A significant reason for the success of most of our actions is commitment, finishing what we started, staying with the decision to its completion. That can only work consistently when we are secure and grounded in our beliefs. When I have no doubt in my motivation, no hesitancy in my execution, and no fear of my outcome then my actions follow instantly, precisely, and completely even under the most difficult of circumstances. Just as Simon and Andrew discovered, it is through these successful habits that we learn to expect positive results and to deal confidently with more and more complex challenges. Only then can we pull the trigger and look forward to the result. Success builds success. Small victories grow into large responsibilities and the fear of failure, that trail of embarrassing compromises, which characterize the lives of so many people, never has to happen. Building a life of faith on the foundation of Christ establishes this confidence, the endurance, and finally the Christian expectation that will leave us eager for life, not reluctant of it. The actions of single moments become a lifetime of significance.

It was just one day, nothing special. The apostle Matthew says it was totally unremarkable, a day like every other, but it was not of their choosing. One day Simon and Andrew were down by the shore practicing their casts, repairing their nets, caulking the boat, checking the weather and the tides, in a word, they were doing their life's work. They were building the skills God had given them, turning action into reflex and preparing themselves for the big one, for the day when that record fish would come along. Ready? They wanted to be more than ready, they wanted to be able to execute perfectly. They were fully committed and determined in their goal. Simon and Andrew considered themselves fishermen and from any perspective you care to take they appeared to be just that.

At about that same time Christ was walking past, he noticed them, their devotion, their readiness for the work that lay ahead, and in an instant, a significant moment to say the least, he called out to them, *"Come, follow me and I will make you fishers of men".*

The Bible says they "left their nets at once" and went with him. They didn't stand around and argue about it, they didn't weigh the pros and cons, or ask a bunch of questions or get emotional about it; they just dropped their stuff and followed. They didn't react, they jumped, and by any other measure that would be a reflex. The story of what followed is the study of the miracle of what God can do with those who are prepared and devoted to life one crucial moment at a time. Their story illustrates the miracle of a single moment becoming a lifetime of significance. Like most of us, they may have begun their day believing that one's significance grows out of one's productivity, or cumulative wealth, or social connections, or any other of the material barometers we often apply to ourselves, but Christ turned that idea upside down when he condensed their entire lifetime into that of a single moment. He took all the moments of their lives up until that point, their hard work, their trials at sea, the storms and the terrors, all the decisions that make a life a life, and he summed them up into one, amazing single act of grace. That moment was their salvation and they accepted it. The lives they lived after that were irrefutably significant.

This remarkable moment out of one unremarkable day promises to all of us that significant moments occur without warning and seldom at the time of our choosing. This miracle in the lives of Simon and Andrew illustrated that in order to respond constructively we must be prepared in advance to respond automatically and reflexively, not influenced by the heat of the moment. Significant moments in our lives are determined by God, not designed or schemed up by us. Our significant choices are carefully fitted to his plan for our lives. Significant moments in our lives lead us to establish significance in the lives of others. By living proactively, and rejecting passivity, we acknowledge that the significant moments in our lives demand total commitment. Once we have turned and are safely on his path there is only one guide to follow and He will lead us to a life of significance.

"I will show you what it's like when someone comes to me, listens to my teaching, and then follows it. It is like a person building a house that digs deep and lays the foundation on solid rock. When the floodwaters rise and break against that house, it stands firm because it's well built."
Luke 6:47-48

"Don't let the excitement of youth cause you to forget your Creator. Honor him in your youth before you grow old and say, "Life is not pleasant anymore."
Ecclesiastes 12:1

Chapter 2

"Take Off the Blinders"

"Satan, who is the god of this world, has blinded the minds of those who don't believe. They are unable to see the glorious light of the Good News. They don't understand the message about the glory of Christ, who is the exact likeness of God."
                              2 Corinthians 4:4

    We are first born of this world, we live our lives bound to it through a physical dependency that creates and reinforces the perception that our reality is one hundred percent earth-based. We see the direct results of our actions, be they successes or failures and quite naturally we assume self-determined responsibility, for the most part never considering any alternative. It is an easy perspective to fall into, and whether life is good or bad, many of us never consider that it could be nothing more than a mirage.
    Satan encourages this blindness, this lie, by focusing man's eyes on the material world, which in turn prioritizes his acts over his faith. It is not so much that men don't want to believe. It is simply that they have been led to believe the wrong things. When man views the world through "old covenant eyes" he sees himself trapped in perpetual sin and he squanders his life through "works" in a failed effort to compensate. This tunnel vision devotion to working out sin hardens a man's mind to his heart so that he cannot hear

God's truth. It is an untrue vision, a ruse offered by Satan and it corrupts the minds of well-intentioned men. This vision becomes the perilous veil that Satan is constantly tending by way of lies and condemnation, and he is more than happy to encourage us to "work" our way to a better life. The fruitless life of toiling away, trying to shovel enough worldly "things" into a bottomless spiritual hole, produces an emptiness that most men cannot articulate. Thoreau correctly identified it as a life of quiet desperation. The vastness of the universe around the man becomes no different than the vastness of the emptiness inside him. Thankfully, but for the grace of God, when man turns through faith and calls on the name of the Lord, this veil is taken away. God lifts the veil and the man's worldly eyes are mercifully focused on the truth. God's infinite truth can then replace man's infinite emptiness.

It is just that simple, a turning, repentance, and an invitation to the Savior who stands at the door and knocks. Paul tells us that those who have had the veil removed can see and reflect the glory of the Lord. They are no longer blinded by Satan's vision and can now see the world as God intended for it to be seen, without shame or conviction.

So, where does this merciful faith come from? How can man be led to the Lord without first being led by someone else? Is it possible that man can "discover" God on his own, through his own physical senses, on his own terms? How do I make it to the Bible, to arrive home in God's word from a position of complete lack of knowledge, of ignorance instilled through a life of worldly experience?

Scripture tells us that ever since the world was created men have pondered the earth and sky. Men have sought to understand and justify them, to explain man's role in them, his reason for being. Scripture tells us that God created the heavens and the earth and everything in them, and through everything God made we can quite clearly see his invisible qualities, his eternal power and divine nature. We have only to consider the vastness of the universe, the complexity of living organisms, the exactitude of the conditions for life, the mighty power of the oceans, the skies and the earth on which we live and it is self-evident that these were not fabricated, nor are they reproducible by man. The heavens proclaim the glory of God; they speak without a sound or word. Yes, they speak rationally to our minds, but more importantly they speak conviction on our hearts. If he once sits down and honestly considers the facts, man has no excuse for not experiencing the presence of God.

The universe did not arise from nothing, it did not come to be but was caused, objects do not move on their own accord but are moved. Chaos does not lead to perfection and perfection is not possible but by design, a rational, intelligent design. Scripture tells us that God's law is written in our hearts and that our own thoughts and conscience convict us or tell us we are doing right. What God lacks in words for the ears registers loudly on the heart. Man has only to muffle his worldly pleas, to refuse Satan's siren song, and God's presence in his heart will speak volumes.

But, the worldly man has traded this truth for a lie. He worships and serves the things God created instead of the creator himself. A man will spend his entire lifetime trying to satisfy his worldly need for things and still remain physically and spiritually empty. The simple truth is, that in order to find God at the center of our universe, we must first dislodge ourselves. We must first stand aside, we must make room, we must finally realize that what's missing is not a physical thing, a momentary thrill, a dominance over others or any of the endless quests that Satan's lies encourage. What is missing is God. The huge hole in the middle of our soul is really no smaller than the vast night sky. It is infinite and unexplainable except through the glory of God. How does man find God? Simple, he must open the eyes to his heart and then he will discover the authentic world, the world filled with God's truth. He must refuse the inward, worldly view offered by Satan and he must look outward with faith.

Satan blinded man to God's glory in the Garden of Eden by enticing Adam and Eve to eat the forbidden fruit. It was this new vision, this new freedom; it was Satan's way of seeing the world that cursed mankind for eternity. It was this veil that has blinded the minds of those who don't believe, and it is this temptation that all men must refuse in order that God's glory can be appreciated. Our mortal dilemma is that although man is capable of acquiring enough knowledge to be able to investigate the world, blinded by this worldly veil, he has been slow to find its creator. He is hampered because he is first borne of this world and destined to view it through worldly eyes.

And who can win this battle against the world? Only those who believe that Jesus is the Son of God. It is only when he is reborn through faith that man is able to know in his heart of God's existence and to truly appreciate the world for which it was intended it to be. In other words, man must first be willing to die a little in order that he may live a lot.

"Instantly something like scales fell from Saul's eyes and he regained his sight. Then he got up and was baptized.
Acts 9:18

CHAPTER 3

"If It's Only Skin Deep"

"When you pray, don't be like hypocrites who love to pray publicly on street corners and in the synagogues where everyone can see them."
                              Matthew 6:5

It was early on in my college career, when learning was not so much for knowledge's sake. It was more like a boot camp on how to slide by. Studying was never about retention, it was just prepping to best the test, and therefore education was for show, not grow. I was a student without a mission, claiming the name while doing everything possible to avoid the responsibility. Unfortunately though, the BS degree in Biology required a basic physics course that I had absolutely no interest in and yet, there it stood like a drooling Doberman, squarely and defiantly in my way. No physics, no degree. No degree, join the Army. I understood the equation, I just couldn't force myself to accept it without a fight, and so I set out with sophomoric intentions to skirt my way around. The course met three mornings a week for one hour with a three hour lab on Friday afternoons, but in those hazy, disjointed days it was far easier just to begin the weekend early, party Thursday night, sleep in, skip class and no-show the lab as well.

Therefore, by the end of our first term the only purpose my textbook had served was as beer-stained coaster for the many malted distractions I consumed, while earnestly defying reality. If there had been extra credit awarded for perpetual levitation of a twelve-ounce can, physics and I would have parted company as quantum friends.

Oh how I defied physics that year. However, of the many laws of classical mechanics I arrogantly rejected, the one that finally drew first blood was, "what goes up, must come down." Newton must have had some jilted cowboy in him, because this deadpan description of gravity suits both planetary motion and the human psyche to a tee. Its undeniable truth echoes the words of one of my favorite country songs, *"Funny how falling feels like flying for a little while."* They're ironic, and poignant, and looking back, I'd give just about anything to have penned them, because I certainly lived them, and when their truth finally roosted home, it was almost too late to recover. So, I'll forever owe a debt of gratitude to an unapologetic physics professor and the "D" he disdainfully shoved my way late one blustery spring afternoon.

There's nothing quite like the brutal honesty of a mirror, the immutable reflection of unfiltered reality, the cold, silent, no-nonsense answer to any challenge you dare to conjure up. My physics professor was just such a device. He saw my name, he considered my work, and he knew I was sitting in his office, longhaired, bare-footed, unkempt, defiant and demanding. He knew me on the surface and was unimpressed. He had no intention of knowing me any further. Yes, we could go on for hours about whose fault that was and how people shouldn't be judged by their outward appearance or behavior or the myriad of other prejudicial subjective standards which can be applied in an unfair style. But, micro-aggression was not a crime in those days, and my indignant expression to him that afternoon was merely one more self-righteous face in an endless line of the dazed and confused. I was just another one of the throng of unfocused, uncommitted, faultless pampered wannabes, looking for a free ride yet complaining when the tires finally went flat. I was a poor excuse for a student and I can't blame him for his unfiltered reflection.

After several rounds of protests, clarifications, explanations and finally my half-baked attempt at begging, the verdict remained unchanged, my "D" was never going anywhere other than onto my permanent, non-negotiable professional transcript. And as bad as that was, the story might have ended right there had not the professor mercifully summed the whole sorry matter up by unknowingly challenging me. His parting, dismissive words were, "You don't deserve any better!"

As I left his office that bare gray, relentless afternoon, retreating angrily through the somber rain, those words rolled over and over again across the shattered image that had earlier reflected my prideful self. Academically and in many other ways I had finally hit bottom, the flying was over and I could either stew there in my own sanctimonious pity, blaming everyone and anything else, or I could start growing for the very first time.

Jesus was well aware of the indolence and shallow commitment we often fall prey to. He used the example of the farmer sowing seed as a metaphor in illustrating God's word and the many difficulties, which can prevent that seed from growing or realizing its fullest potential. Like seed that lands on a well-worn footpath only to be immediately trampled, the word can be intercepted by the devil and taken from our hearts outright, thus denying any chance of acceptance and salvation. Or, like seed sown in rocky soil which can't take root, his word can make it into the heart, but lacking cooperation and conviction on our part, never grow strong enough to survive life's trials and temptation. The word can also suffer like seed, which falls among thorns, received initially with conviction and yet unknowingly crowded out of the heart by the cares and riches and pleasures of this world. Mercifully though, seed, which falls on good soil, will flourish and prosper just like the word, which finds repentant hearts and grows with abundance through the lives of those who hear it, cling to it, and obey it without reserve.

In a sense, reflecting back on those misspent days in college, this parable is all about my devotion to embracing the word, not rejecting it. It's about my strength of faith, not rebellion. It's about allowing God's word to grow and to root deeply into my heart. It's not about a superficial or pretentious faith that flourishes today and then is gone tomorrow. God's word cannot be treated as a passive, take it or leave it influence in our lives.

Like my physics book, I can't just set the Bible on the dusty desk and expect, that some miraculous process, impart its message into my heart. I must be an intentional partner. As powerful as it is, the influence of God's word in my life is only as strong as the commitment I am willing to give it. Like my physics course, the lesson was never about the easy way around, instead, it was all about the narrow gate. God's word, unlike the laws of physics, cannot be overcome or circumvented through the wiles of men.

Finally, rather like my physics professor, God does not accept a superficial understanding or shallow faith. In fact, he rejects it outright. So, wouldn't it be a blessing to be able to look in the mirror one day and have a confidant face stare back, to be judged not dismissively but with praise? Joshua got it and left us these directions. His faith was not just skin deep. He was simply all in.

"For my part, I wholeheartedly followed the Lord my God."
Joshua 14:8

CHAPTER 4

"Second Chance"

"The faithful love of the Lord never ends! His mercies never cease. Great is his faithfulness; his mercies begin afresh each morning."
Lamentations 3:22-23

    I can't count the number of times I've made a snap decision or reacted to some sudden urgent situation without really considering the consequences, only to find myself later, "up the river without a paddle". Inevitably, at some unexpected, out-of-control moment each of us has probably suffered circumstances for which we saw no clear way past, no escape. That's life, right? But all it takes is a near-death experience, an epiphany of lifestyle, or an illness with no apparent cure and that infinite horizon of cozy possibilities, which usually marks our everyday lives, is urgently and fearfully winnowed down to the very next and maybe last precious moment.
    So, isn't it ironic that we have this odd way of insulating ourselves from the raw enormity of such crises? It defies logic why those first few minutes which follow, often spent praising our good fortune, while at the same time denouncing our miserable luck, becomes less and less acute as each new second ticks blissfully by. But, while we often wryly boast that whatever doesn't kill you only leaves you stronger, it's unfortunate that what does go unreconciled is this ironic, new-found

courage, a courage which leaves us more brazen than ever before. The sad result is that one's spiritual vulnerability is gradually heightened through the habit of steady self-centered desensitization, and every time we jump over the fire unscathed it only makes our next approach that much more daring. Invincibility fosters self-reliance and gradually we become godless masters of the universe. Martin Luther observed it this way,

"When we are in danger, our fear is without measure. But once the danger is past, we imagine it to have been less than it was. This is the delusion of Satan, to diminish and obscure the grace of God".

He viewed our problem as being far more complex than just a material crisis. He correctly focuses our attention by identifying it as a stealthy assault on spiritual resolve. This all too human response to an unannounced confrontation with mortality can both humble us and jade us. The first and natural impression is, "Thank God, I'm alive", but our next words too often are, "Now, show me what you've really got." Adrenaline can be that visceral. It's all about fight or flight, and when dire circumstances don't immediately resume, it's not long before our respect for them selfishly and pridefully abates. In some defiant and incomprehensible way we somehow convince ourselves that good fortune is unquestionably the result of our own adroit skill, superior intelligence, or sacrificial offering despite the aroma of fear and mortality that lingers. Our ignorance, denial and pride coalesce into the same smug grin you might see worn by the man who has just stepped out of a haystack he landed on after falling from the sky without a parachute. So how does that happen, how do I maintain a calm demeanor in the light of an undeniable and uncontrollable fate? How can I possibly explain grace without acknowledging and embracing its true source? How do we recognize and honor the legitimate source of our second chances?

David was not confused. He put it this way, "What if the Lord had not been on our side?" Psalm One hundred and twenty-four greets us with this simple question and then, as if to encourage the reader to pause and let the words burrow in, the writer asks again, "What if the Lord had not been on our side?" It's not often that we are faced with a rhetorical confrontation in scripture, especially in such an incisive and emphatic way. David's immediate and convenient response to the question is that God's benevolence is to rescue us from the overwhelming traps of life. A no-nonsense answer to a provocative question to be sure. The psalmist's words are unexpected, the psalm itself is fairly short, the answer is succinct, and if my thoughts are attuned strictly to material peril, the answer is more than sufficient. It was just another close call, right? Without warning we were challenged with an innocent question and the convenient response rescued us from having to delve any deeper.

The superficial reader might blow right through this thinking, "Whew, I'm glad I didn't have to reflect on that one long, what's the big idea anyway asking loaded questions?" But isn't that just what Martin Luther warned us of? Somehow we stumbled into this unexpected challenge and just as quickly the solution materialized, neat and sweet. So, bolstered with unfounded confidence we sped off on our merry way, never really appreciating the opportunity for its worth. All along though, the author's true desire, just like Martin Luther advised, was to encourage us to look beyond worldly significance and to focus intentionally on the spiritual application. And not surprisingly, rather than lazily settling on the convenient response, if I explore a little further, David warns me in Psalm One hundred and twenty-seven,

"Unless the Lord builds a house, the work of the builders is wasted. Unless the Lord protects a city, guarding it with sentries will do no good. It is useless for you to work so hard from morning until late at night, anxiously working for food to eat, for God gives rest to his loved ones."

Basically, what he is teaching me is that I can make all the plans I want, build the finest, biggest house in the neighborhood, surround myself with all the material protection and insurance money can buy, and commit all my life energies into doing so, but if the Lord is not on my side it will all be wasted, it will do no good. If my plans do not have God's stamp of approval they really are not plans at all. Shakespeare's immortal description of a man's lack of divine purpose said it best, "Life's but a walking shadow, a poor player that struts and frets his hour upon the stage and then is heard no more. It is a tale told by an idiot, full of sound and fury signifying nothing." Isn't a life spent careening from one crisis to another, never fully appreciating purpose or design, just an empty life, a walking shadow? In order to realize purpose in life don't we have to base it in something that makes sense, don't we have to have God on our side.

    Second chances are all about perspective and repentance. If we fail to recognize them for the opportunity they really are - the priceless chance to begin anew - then perhaps we are full of sound and fury. Certainly a life without God on our side signifies nothing. Second chances should be the time for pause, for rededication, for introspection. Second chances should not be about a furtive sigh of relief. Rather they should be the celebration of faith, the recognition of God's design in our lives. They should be a grateful promise to do it right this time.

    When God is on my side I don't fear the fickle nature of chance, I know I have been graced with The Second Chance and I live in the hope and confidence that it provides. Perhaps a second chance is God's way of turning me away from my prideful walk and pointing me down His path. Then all I have to do is wake up.

"When the Lord brought back his exiles to Jerusalem, it was like a dream! We were filled with laughter, and we sang for joy."
                                                                Psalm 126:1-2

CHAPTER 5

"Choices"

Jesus told them, "This is the only work God wants from you; believe in the one he has sent."
                                                        John 6:29

    I grew up in a modest, middle-class neighborhood. We had simple needs and, for the most part, only simple problems. Seldom was there ever any call for a critical decision. As a product of post-war America, I was insulated and over-protected from the realities of life that patiently waited on my eventual collision with the world. My childhood friends suffered right along with me in this antiseptic neutrality which we came to trust and rely on, and despite the undeniable traumas which hovered around us, we grew up blandly unconcerned and totally naive to the crucial decisions which would eventually confront us. The sad, ironic effect of this cocoon on my spiritual maturity was almost catastrophic considering the noble intentions from which it arose.

    My parents and the parents of most of my friends viewed this shield as their civic duty. It was their simple compensation for the traumas they themselves had experienced while living their own generational struggles through world war, the threat of nuclear holocaust and the faceless, ever present political threats, which promised to upend their own humble notions of an ideal life. The bottom line is that we grew up never really appreciating the true weight of choice - the weight that is represented in one's soul. We were never empowered to finally and irrevocably decide on just about anything, and the terrible consequence is that many of us never achieved the far-sighted vision that choice demands, especially the self-denial, and often times uncomfortable conclusions, that crucial decisions necessarily produce. We grew up averse to unpleasant truths and blind to the dead-ends that bad choices, or even no choice at all, could lead to. Admittedly, I was particularly oblivious in my own self-absorbed state, and when the moment came for me to seriously decide, I was pretty much blind to the weight this moment demanded.

    Every year since high school, a group of my friends has managed to reunite for a golf outing, some fellowship, and oftentimes for honest, open conversations about what it means to be a man in the ever-changing world, the world that seems to promise one thing but almost always delivers something else. Not unexpectedly these conversations often revolve around the choices we made, good or bad, the troubles that eventually boiled out of them, and what would they have done in another's shoes. You can't open up like this to just anybody, so it helps knowing the brother that you are confessing to has carried the same or similar baggage.
    Our gatherings usually begin with a reminder in the form of an email or phone call, always with the same old request. Do you plan to be here this year? It's a simple choice, right? But then, once you

figure in the interruptions to your preferred routine or the interference with some other plan or activity that you were already gearing up for, the choice often becomes a nagging headache.

    Despite the fact that you've known about this day all year long, you put it off hoping something else will come along that can give you halfway acceptable cover not to accept, but that never really happens. So then comes the follow up call, the unavoidable moment of truth when you either have to give in and accept, or fabricate some crisis that even a child could see through. So you suck up the ten pounds you gained since the last outing, brush the few unruly hairs you still have left proclaiming your manhood, dust the mold off your clubs and make the reluctant drive yet one more time knowing all along that it was the smartest decision you could have made all year.

    Critical choices are like that. They showcase two competing voices, one screaming at the top of his lungs for attention, and the other just patiently waiting his turn. Unfortunately, these two voices are lifelong mortal enemies, and our choices inevitably reflect their titanic struggle for the soul of a man. One is the "good ole me" voice, the quasi-contented, been bought off so many times you can't count voice, the voice that promises to shut up immediately if you will just lay down on the couch, turn on the TV and put your mind on pause until all the dust settles. It's the silky smooth, manipulative voice of sacrifice, as in it will sacrifice you all day long just to have its one-track, prideful way. The "good ole me" voice is all about self and never about anything or anyone else. It's a superficial voice that denies alternatives because it never sees a situation from any perspective other than itself. It's a voice without ears. To be honest, it's a dead-end voice, but so many of us would rather lie on the dead-end couch than get up and answer the door that it's a voice with huge momentum and authority. Selfishly taking the path of least resistance, most of us eventually condition ourselves to give in to it. It speaks me, it knows me, it promises me, it represents me, but if I'm completely truthful, it's really not about me at all.

The other voice is that quiet, humble voice, the soft voice of reason. It is my lone true advocate. It's a patient voice, infinitely and mercifully patient. It must be so in order to be heard above the fury concocted by its counterpart. The steady voice of reason is often no voice at all, but more like an intuition, a hint. It's a barely discernible warning, like the feeling you have before something really unwanted happens. And although faint, it is so incisive and brutally honest that once I sense it everything else grinds to a halt in order to listen. Unfortunately, the voice of reason often defaults to the voice of last resort, to be considered only when all else has failed and I've exhausted every other excuse. It's the voice that never lies, but because it is the voice of obedience, for most of us it becomes the voice of dread, so we tend to ignore it. Mercifully though, the voice of reason is always there to take you back, like a loving father, to pick up the pieces and set you rightfully on your way.

So you made the commitment to show up. You've calculated the cost of time off work, greens fees, the embarrassment of having to perform in the presence of your most critical judges, and a myriad of other minor nuisances that dissuaded those others who failed to show. In accepting this challenge you've demonstrated a little mastery over the selfish voice and a hopeful show of obedience to the voice of reason. Of course, remaining neutral was never an option, that would have been a decision not to choose, and in effect, accepting whatever might happen. Leaving choice to the vagaries of chance is not why man was entrusted with free will. Basically, to refuse to choose is to refuse to be a man.

The decision to play was a simple answer to a simple problem and if all our choices were that simple life would be easier than golf, right? So what's the connection? What's the logic between a simple material choice on the surface and this huge spiritual struggle that sits just below? How do I dare give equal weight to two entirely opposite questions in my life, one seemingly unimportant and the other crucially so? How do I sell the connection between a simple everyday invitation and the most critical one in my life?

The short answer is that a decision which leads to either choice is, and always will be, represented by the same two voices that have wrestled for my soul my entire life, my two old buddies, the hollow boast of pride and the humble voice of faith. It is how I weight those two voices in each and every decision that I will ever make which determines not only my future, but also just as importantly, the future of those whom I live to influence.

As it turns out, my private decisions are never an isolated event. Donne said it best, "No man is an island." Each and every choice I make in life is observed and considered by others, whether I like it or not, whether I am aware of it or not, and those who witness my choices are in turn influenced by them. The two voices that constantly struggle for my attention are no different from the two that struggle for everyone else's. The appeals they make to me are the same they make to each and every one of us. It's an ancient battle, this titanic struggle for self and the arguments those two make have been honed down through generations of clueless men to efficient perfection. There is no unique set of circumstances that set my life, or the trials I encounter, apart from anyone else's. Yes, we each walk a different path, but that path still carries us through the same world, the same troubles, the same doubts and fears, the same mortal destiny, and ultimately to the same critical moment of choice.

The problem is that if my life has grown nonchalant to choice, or if I have become the product of choices governed by superficial concerns or isolation, either willful or through circumstances not immediately under my control, then the result is likely to be the wrong response when that critical moment finally arrives. Jesus said that the *"only act God asks of you is to believe in the One he has sent"*. He also said, *"Look, I stand at the door and knock. If you hear my voice and open the door, I will come in and we will share a meal together as friends."* The choice is simple, "Do I open the door? Do I believe?

It's almost too incredible to accept that we are placed in this glorious Eden in order to be prepared for one simple but profound decision, a decision that has such enormous consequence, and yet that choice is seldom seen for what it is until much too late. Many of us become complacent through worldly diversions and the multitude of complexities that characterize our frenetic lives. We become steadily desensitized to the weight that one critical choice can carry or somehow convince ourselves that it can be safely put off to another day. But that's the selfish voice speaking, the laissez-faire voice of cool, the noncommittal shrug of men who have been cynically lied to and shepherded by a dead-end material world.

We read in Luke that the rich man realized this way too late. In a poignant plea that will resound for eternity he begged Abraham to warn his brothers. The terrible consequence of his wasted selfish life became not only his eternal separation from God, but sadly, it destined his family to follow him right along. His thoughtless choices became their eternal grief. Scripture tells us we are instructed to teach our families of their impending danger. And further, we are specifically warned that failure to do so could result not only in their deaths but ours as well. Their spiritual deaths then become our personal responsibility. That's a sober thought to consider. That's the real problem with poor choices, especially when they are made for selfish reasons. You could argue that each man has the right, as well as the free will, to decide for himself the eventual fate of his own soul, but when you finally realize and admit that this choice cannot be made in isolation, it suddenly takes on a whole new meaning.

It's amazing, the feeling that passes over when a great decision has been made. Make's you want to crow about it. It's like a huge weight has been lifted, which is the exact opposite to the load you felt when you continued to carry that burden. The psalmist put it this way, *"He has given me a new song to sing, a hymn of praise to our God. Many will see what he has done and be amazed. They will put their trust in the Lord."* That's what this life is all about. Making a remarkable choice and letting others know about it, letting them see that they might know as well. That's the choice that matters most in life and, in fact, it is life. And like the good book says, live it abundantly.

"Believe in the Lord Jesus Christ and you will be saved, along with everyone in your household."
                                                        Acts 16:31

CHAPTER 6

"What Is Truth?"

"You say I am a king. Actually, I was born and came into the world to testify to the truth. All who love the truth recognize that what I say is true". "What is truth?" Pilate asked. Then he went out again to the people and told them, "He is not guilty of any crime".

John 18:37-38

When was the last time you found yourself in a discussion with someone and you were defending what you "knew" was a superior position. Yet, deep down inside you sensed there might be a flaw in your reasoning at some critical level, but the idea that you were advocating was so appealing that you just couldn't resist the effort. At some point you were likely telling yourself something like this, "If I carry this point long enough eventually one of two things is gonna happen, either I will discover what it is that makes it true or I'll bamboozle the person I'm talking to into believing me anyway - and in a sense, that will make it true, so either way I win!" It's a common situation I'm sure and it goes to the heart of the story that follows, because no matter how we try to spin the it, truth is always in the eyes of the beholder. Or is it?

As the story goes, four blind men were offered a challenge. The rules were fairly simple. Identify an object placed before you and collect one million dollars, no questions asked. The only condition was that in order to take the "Test" each man had to wager his life savings, he had to risk it all. So just to sweeten the deal, the offer was amended to provide a payout of one million dollars a year for life. It seemed a relatively small wager considering the inestimable payout, so four random guys were asked and each of them, having little to no savings, eagerly accepted.

The test was straightforward. The men were led into a large, cavernous room and placed randomly around an elephant. Yes, a large, quiet, unmoving, neutral-smelling elephant. Each man was then asked in turn to identify the object before him. The first man, standing squarely in front of the elephant grabbed his trunk and after carefully examining it pronounced it to be a heavy gauge pipe. Accurately sensing the large space he was standing in, the first blind man stated, "I have no doubt we have been placed in a mechanical room and this is some sort of conduit, it is warm so it must carry hot water or gas, maybe it's a steam pipe".

The second man, who was standing directly behind the elephant, grabbed his long brushy tail and after a few strained moments weighing the possibilities he finally announced, "I am absolutely confident that this is a broom of some sort, attached no doubt to a mechanical cleaning device, probably an industrial warehouse sweeper considering the large space we are standing in".

The third blind man was standing at one of the elephant's legs, but stretching as much as he could, he was unable to reach around the full girth. However, correctly assessing it to be a large circular-shaped vertical structure, he deduced it to be a column. "A support column for a large underground space, probably a parking deck or foundational pillar", he confidently asserted.

Finally, the fourth blind man, who had been placed to the side, planted his hands confidently on the elephant's flank and after feeling the rough, bumpy expanse stretched out before him, deliberated for less than a minute and jubilantly announced, "This is a solid rock wall, no doubt about it. We're standing in the atrium of some huge hotel or bank building, and if it's a bank like I think it is, I'll take my money now thank-you!"

Trusting solely their physical senses and rational intellect, each man in turn made his confident assessment, and each man in turn failed absolutely. So, just to give them a fighting chance the patient examiner encouraged the four blind men to consult with one another to make one final deliberation as to the identity of the item before them. To make the offer even more attractive he doubled the original terms, two million dollars a year for life to each man. As you might have surmised by now, try as they might there was no common ground. Each man, assured of his own view of the "truth", either exhausted himself trying to convince the others or resorted to being obstinate when another view was presented. The result was four convictions with no shared belief, no truth that was consistent to every situation.

Each man was essentially speaking a foreign language to his neighbor. Each man suffered from an identical handicap, the inability to "see the truth", and worse, they failed to appreciate the peril that deficiency really implied. They were so confident in their self-reliance and so focused on the potential material reward that they refused to consider the problem through a different perspective. Secretly, each man was smug in his own assessment and no matter what the others argued, there was really no compromise. As it turns out, because there were no other rules, all they ever had to do was ask the examiner and he would have given them the answer.

Aren't we all so guilty of that? When our minds are inside the bottle looking out, the perspective is always tiny compared to what lies outside. So what can I do, how do I hope to understand the unfathomable? How do I get outside the bottle? Or viewed a little differently, is it really fair to ask a blind person to see? Is it fair to be confronted with a question that we are so ill equipped as men to consider? The Bible says of course, that's really the only way; the hard part is managing the blinders.

Scripture tells us that Pilate was a mediocre Roman governor faced with a no-win decision, which he resented and attempted to circumvent, but God's plan was already in motion and like Judas he was destined to play his part. Strictly from the evidence, Christ was not guilty of breaking any Roman law, certainly none punishable by death, but Pilate had no intention of being complicit in any rash Jewish legal decisions, especially just prior to the Passover, so he practically begged Jesus to acquit himself. As a provincial administrator Pilate's personal view of truth was jaded both by the bureaucratic system he oversaw as well as the relentless stream of hardened criminals who were dragged before him boasting of their innocence. In his world truth was contrived, it was convenient, and it was relative. Those properties alone were enough to render him deaf when the authentic Truth finally addressed him. But the time had come for men to face the truth, or at least to put a clock on choosing one's side, and in those final oppressive moments before Christ was flogged and crucified, Pilate muttered the most monumental question of all, "What is truth?"

You might say his question reflected an exasperation of the circumstances, or a sarcastic appraisal of their conversation. Some have suggested it was the acerbic pessimism of a man who had been lied to one too many times, or maybe even an urgent, honest repentant plea. Regardless, we will never know, but without waiting for a response, Pilate immediately turned Jesus over to the mob and charged them to levy a verdict. It was during these brief critical moments that we witness three disparate perspectives of truth, not by coincidence but specifically in order to frame the one that matters most. In this final climactic exchange we hear Truth as the word of God. We hear the truth as one man's version, and we hear the truth as a societal construct, a verdict.

Jesus first states, *"You say I am a king. Actually I was born and came into the world to testify to the truth"*. Then we hear Pilate, acting from his own personal agenda and biases make this deliberation: "He is not guilty of any crime. But you have a custom of asking me to release one prisoner each year at Passover. Would you like me to release this King of the Jews?" And lastly, we hear the mob render their version of the truth when they shout back as one,"No, not this man. We want Barabbas!"

The Truth stood before them all, but like the four blind men, either independently or as one, both Pilate and the mob failed to see it. So what do these three contradictory forms of the truth imply, what significance do they play in my life, and most importantly, which one is the only truth that matters?

As worldly beings we are challenged to manage truth through one or more of these three lenses, each of them constantly competing for attention; truth at the personal, subjective, individual level, truth as a conceptual social construct, a politically correct truth, and truth as God's word, the Gospel. It seems so obvious as to which is the only one trustworthy, authentic source but the material world has a way of lending credence to each of the others, so much so that their roar often silences the lone voice of eternal reason.

It is because we are compelled to view life through the unique and finite series of experiences that shape each of us that a subjective, personal, assessment of reality or truth is by definition impossible for any other human being to share completely. In a sense, an individual's version of the truth corresponds to a private reality, much like the truth of the self-reliant man or the stoic. Truth at the personal level is just that, it's personal, and any interpretation achieved by others is just that, an interpretation, hardly a basis for foundational belief. Like Pilate's declaration of Christ's innocence, it is merely one man's best guess, flavored by his circumstances, and should carry no more weight than that.

Although more comprehensive, because it profits from the input of many individuals, the cultural or group concept of truth suffers from flexibility and becomes too broad. By design it reflects social conformity, and because the group concept of truth must provide a generic application, inevitably it is deficient at the individual level. The group concept of truth embraces relativity in order to encompass universal application and therefore effectively endorses nothing. Societal truth becomes a moment-by-moment dynamic phenomenon without foundation. In simple terms, in attempting to please everyone, cultural truth fulfills no one, and just like the trial scene above, mob rule inevitably leads away from truth and to poor decisions.

The bottom line is that mankind, whether alone or in groups can neither interpret nor describe truth in all of its infinite glory. That job was far too important for worldly men with worldly vision. Scripture warns us that the Truth cannot be found in our own hearts and that whatever we "know" through the world actually corrupts us. Scripture also tells us that the Truth came in the form of Jesus Christ; it is God's word. It is His law. Neither as individuals nor as a civilization can man deduce godly truth, but we continue to try. In order to know the truth we must live in the word and we must want to do the will of God. So practically speaking, how do I know godly truth?

Well, it helps to know what it is not. Worldly truth placates, it vacillates and distorts over time. Godly truth is a rock. Worldly truth patronizes and disables, like a siren it is pleasing to the ears. Godly truth bypasses the senses and, like a two-edged sword, goes straight to the soul. Worldly truth pits men against each other. Godly truth draws men together. Worldly truth is often the first idea that pops up, but it never sees you through. Godly truth is eternal. Worldly truth was designed by man. Godly truth existed before man. Worldly truth is impatient, unloving, and unreliable. Godly truth celebrated the return of the prodigal son. Worldly truth reflects the laws of man and rejects the laws of God. Worldly truth is fear. Godly truth is grace. Worldly truth stood face to face with God and was blind. Godly truth removed the scales from Paul's eyes. Worldly truth insists that blind men go it alone. Godly truth is just a prayer away. Worldly truth leaves men in darkness. Godly truth is a lamp unto your feet. Worldly truth insists on conformity. Godly truth promises to set you free.

"I am the light of the world. If you follow me you will not have to walk in darkness, because you will have the light that leads to life".
John 8:12

CHAPTER 7

"Lead Courageously"

"So fear the Lord and serve him wholeheartedly. Put away forever the idols your ancestors worshipped when they lived beyond the Euphrates River and in Egypt. Serve the Lord alone. But if you refuse to serve the Lord, then choose today whom you will serve. Would you prefer the gods your ancestors served beyond the Euphrates? Or will it be the gods of the Amorites in whose land you now live? But as for me and my family, we will serve the Lord".
Joshua 24:14-15

Life is finally a test of stewardship, the sum of whatever confronts us with whatever our response turns out to be, how we reconcile our circumstances to our gifts. It is earnestly accepting responsibility. Life demands we manage not only our immediate personal needs and wants, but that this management be consistent with and in concert with God's world around us. Although self-preservation is hard-wired into our genes, altruism, humility and self-sacrifice are equally important. Scripture warns us that, *"God is not mocked: for whatsoever a man soweth, that shall he also reap."*

Therefore, we are responsible for our actions, and like it or not, all actions have consequences. Ultimately, everything we undertake affects those around us. Some would protest, "That's not fair, I didn't choose these circumstances, they chose me,

I have every right to go about my life as I see fit, not tailored or limited in any way by the endless procession of people and their problems that I come in contact with. If I don't want to be responsible I don't have to." But can anyone ever remain totally isolated? Short of being shipwrecked on a deserted island the odds of complete isolation are pretty much nil, therefore most of us are led by necessity to adopt some basic leadership and stewardship skills. No man is an island, and even if we could refuse to inspire others, still we remain to be inspired in ourselves.

Now assuming that the majority of us seek a favorable return for any investment in effort we might make, it pays to give considerable attention to stewardship, for the time and life resources that we expend are truly precious. The real bottom line is that all behavior, whether good or bad, advantageous or not will be rewarded eventually, and how we lead will determine where we arrive.

So, do I lead with conviction, courageously, or do I abdicate and follow irresponsibly? The answers to these questions will reflect my stewardship, and more importantly they will reflect the personal standards from which they arise. It seems ironic, but in order to lead courageously we must first have the courage to be led, and to be led in faith. Paul said it this way, "God's intent was that now, through the church, the manifold wisdom of God should be made known." In the end leadership becomes an amalgamation of three basic but essential factors in our lives: what we are made of, what we are molded by, and what we mean to others. In other words, the combination of our intrinsic self - the person God designed for earthly life, our extrinsic self - the person shaped and sharpened through Christian discipleship, and the purpose-bound self - the man God has prepared as an example to influence others.

In 1637 the French philosopher Rene Descartes famously deduced, "I think, therefore I am". In making this declaration Descartes was affirming the direct, immutable connection between his freewill mind and the life he lived, the actions he undertook, his intrinsic self. Not only was he proclaiming his unique, God-gifted life, he was also accepting personal responsibility. In just three immortal words Descartes forever separated man from the excuse of his deterministic past. Man was no longer a puppet, but a free-willed individual. It follows then that a man's responsibility arises from the essential understanding that one's actions must be consistent with one's freewill beliefs. Therefore, a man's resolute core beliefs must reflect his absolute faith. James insisted that absolute faith would always inspire passionate acts. Paul later wrote, "I am obligated, I am unashamed, and I am eager". He too recognized that great leaders ultimately lead through what they believe in, what they have resolved to stand for, and what they are determined to suffer for.

It is so true that for all too many of us we are our own worst enemy, our intrinsic self is inconsistent with what we aspire to be. But is that really the case? Far too often I have set out with good intentions only to revert back to my old sinful ways, and the problem is not so much the sin, for I can never be sinless, it is the false notion that I can master that sin alone. Paul put it this way, "I have discovered this principle of life, that when I want to do right, I inevitably do what is wrong. I love God's Law with all my heart. But there is another power within me that is at war with my mind. This power makes me a slave to the sin that is still within me". As sinners, we suffer a lifelong struggle, a dogfight, between our faith in the Word and the siren call of the world. For the most part it is a private, lonely war, fought on unfamiliar turf that is better known by Satan than we ourselves. But it does not have to be. God has prepared a way and he has blessed us with a remarkable friend.

    Just as Christ responded confidently in the wilderness and Paul withstood years of solitude productively in prison, great leaders do what's right even when they are alone, even when there are no witnesses other than one's conscience and the Holy Spirit. In all cases, the crucial difference between success and failure is faith in God's word, it is leading not through self-reliance, but through the strength of faith, it is rebutting the material world with God's word, it is walking with courage in the light that promises to lead us.

    Leaders are constantly molded by circumstances and conditions outside or extrinsic to their core being as well. But it is not so much the nature of the challenge as it is the response or adaptation to it that separates courageous leaders from those who fall short. Scripture tells us that,

"The heart of man plans his way, but the Lord establishes his steps". Courageous is the man who steps up and embraces the trials and challenges that God sets before him, rather than denying their source and resorting to a self-reliant or defiant stance. Having once placed his fate in the hands of Christ, the successful leader can venture beyond his shadow and respond to challenges with a power and strength that comes only from the Holy Spirit.

Leaders are made then, they are not just born. They are made by hard effort, which is the price all of us must pay to achieve any goal that is worthwhile. James encourages us with these promising words, "Blessed is the man who remains steadfast under trial, for when he has stood the test he will receive the crown of life, which God has promised to those who love him". Like Peter, James was a man of action, he wore his faith on his chest and he was not afraid to fail. All he really ever asked for was one more chance. If you listen carefully you can just imagine either man picking himself up from another dusting and with conviction declaring, "Sir, thank you Sir, may I have another Sir! Those are the words of a courageous leader, enduring in spite of circumstances, ever rising to the occasion, and most importantly, willing to be led, to be obedient.

Lastly, courageous leaders lead by example rather than command. They combine the strengths they are made of with the powers they are molded by and they share it with those whom they influence. They live out God's plan for their lives. They are not afraid to call out the phonies. They stick up for their people and most important of all, they are servants. Christ challenged his disciples, "It is not this way among you, but whoever wishes to become great among you shall be your servant". How ironic it is that we must first submit before we can lead, but isn't that what it is all about?

In order that we may lead the lives God has intended for us to lead we must first realize and accept that we are not the leader but His follower, and that the only correct or righteous path is the one God has laid out for us, not the one we have planned on our own. That realization takes courage, but most of all it takes humility, the kind of humility that always puts the house of the Lord before that of man.

"And why have I called you for this work? Why did I call you by name when you did not know me? It is for the sake of Jacob my servant, Israel my chosen one".
Isaiah 45:4

"For the kingdom of God is not just a lot of talk, it is living by God's power".
1Corinthians 4:20

CHAPTER 8

"Why Should I Want Eternal Life?"

"If a man dies, will he live again? All the days of my hard service I will wait for my renewal to come. You will call and I will answer you; you will long for the creature your hands have made. Surely then you will count my steps but not keep track of my sin".
Job 14:14-16

What a loaded question, "Why should I want eternal life?" Job looked at it from two angles. He assumed that his creator would surely "long for the creature" his hands had made, therefore even after his "hard service" had ended he would be renewed, God would bring him back. He was thinking it really wasn't a matter of his choice that God was planning all along to have him live again. Job's main concern was not whether or not he would be restored, but to what circumstances. His worry was that God would not credit him with the good works in his life, but rather punish him for the sins. In Job's day the concept of life after death was associated more with punishment than reward, so his perception was, that in spite of all the suffering he had endured, death might not offer relief but only commit him to even more. He was anxious and saw no end to it, and when you consider the trials and misery that Job eventually survived, you can begin to appreciate his worry. Job was not so sure he wanted to live again. He was convinced that God was a vindictive god without mercy or any capacity for empathy, and that he was just a helpless victim, a pawn in a tragic drama for which there was no hope or recourse.

Unfortunately, this is the opinion that many people have when they weigh the relative meaninglessness of their lives against the idea of a capricious and distant God. They view the potential of eternal life and life after death as just an extension of "more of the same". Their immediate worldly concerns negate any chance of spiritual growth and the result is a permanent, eternal, self-imposed separation from God. Job was handicapped in much the same sense except for one, big, critical difference - he began his trials with faith in God, and God never left his side. The important "take away" to Job's story is that in spite of all his trials, he never abandoned his faith, he never left God, and he never allowed his worldly misery to overwhelm his spiritual determination. The result of this trust was even more amazing.

Scripture reveals two major themes regarding eternal life, the first is that life-after-death is an eternal heavenly state, a perfect, timeless adoration of God in the presence of God. This is the eternity we think of first, the eternity of Matthew and John prior to their walk with Christ. It is a concept steadily revealed through the Old Testament and fulfilled in the New Testament. It is a picture of heaven that begins in shadowy uncertainty but grows to glorious celebration. It is an eternity that becomes more inviting and rewarding as our understanding of God unfolds.

The second theme is subtler. It is the essential life-after-rebirth. The life in faith we are to live now on earth. Most of us, and that included Job, believe that eternal life applies strictly to what follows after we have walked our days on earth, but the Bible, specifically the Gospel, promises so much more. If we define our understanding of eternal life incorrectly as God's reward for Christian living or as an enticement to salvation then we will have overlooked the most important aspect of all, and that is eternal life as a calling, as the life God seeks from us today. Eternal life then becomes God's own life living in us, and as we have been born again in Christ, this new life will last forever. Eternal life in this capacity celebrates our re-birth and reveals the Christ within us. This is the life that we display in drawing others to Christ, in being a part of the body of Christ, in justifying the free will of our mortal selves. Eternal life becomes the state of being in the present, of reflecting the rejection of our old selves and the celebration of our new, it is knowing Christ, it is preparing for our heavenly eternal life, it is everlasting life.

Like Job, people are often led to deny faith simply because they do not find the prospect of eternal life attractive. Actually, what they mistakenly fear is not an eternal life in the biblical sense, but a continuation of their present material life. That false assumption naturally encourages the universal human desire to postpone death for as long as possible. An eternal material life is presumed to result in unending monotony and therefore unbearable. So, to continue living forever appears to be more a curse than a gift. When we take that short-sighted position, what we fail to realize is that everything that makes us enjoy life as it is finds its fundamental source in God. God is the One who made enjoyment, the one who made this Earth, and therefore, what is in it is a reflection of His goodness and beauty. All that is good, admirable, and enjoyable finds its ultimate source in God. Sin has abused it, twisted it, and skewed it to give us short-term pleasure bound to a life that will inevitably cause harm.

It's unfortunate, but in missing this incredible opportunity to live in Christ, too many people have come to know the Lord and received forgiveness of their sins, only to remain spiritually stagnant, saved but stuck. They mistakenly await heaven so that then and only then can they begin eternal living, but this is missing the main point of salvation. If all you have done is believe in Christ so you won't perish, then you have denied yourself the opportunity to share the everlasting life that God wishes for you right now. It was this old covenant view of sin-based eternity that had Job blinded to the redeemed eternal life in Christ his spirit longed for. Although he raged against the terrible trials of his life, somewhere deep inside Job never lost this faith, and because of that unyielding spirit God ultimately blessed him.

Perhaps the better question is not so much "Why should I want eternal life?" but rather, "How can my life today become eternal?" Once you understand that true eternal life begins with a personal relationship with Christ, it leads to the more important question, and that is, "How do I begin?" That's the question with the beautiful lifesaving answer. Eternal life means escaping the power of death, the life that is ruled by death. Everything that lives will die. But, scripture tells us that death wasn't the end for Jesus. God brought him back to life, and his resurrection defeated death. In the same way, death isn't the end of the story for us. The way to eternal life is to know Christ. To know Christ is to be led along the path of everlasting life. When Jesus said eternal life is to know God, he was speaking of having an intimate, close, personal relationship with God. Eternal life also refers to the quality of this life. Jesus said, *"I came that they may have life, and have it abundantly"*. This was one of the main differences between the early church and the church of today. It was the story of Job. They knew God intimately, they had a relationship with the Lord that wasn't waiting to start in heaven, but was working in them while they were still in this world. Why live a short life of pleasure but an eternity apart from God when you can have an eternity with the God who loves you and created all that is good in the first place, both today and tomorrow?

"And this is the way to have eternal life - to know you, the only true God, and Jesus Christ, the one you sent to earth".
John 17:3

CHAPTER 9

"Partnering With God"

"I no longer call you slaves, because a master does not confide in his slaves. Now you are my friends, since I have told you everything the Father told me. You didn't choose me. I chose you.
John 15:15-16

    My mother was a Christian, but she was also a lifelong smoker. The cancer had spread to both her liver and brain when we first discovered it and the treatment was really only palliative from that point. The one drug that offered any curative effect caused more discomfort than she could bear, and so we had to accept the inevitable and make the best of her remaining days. Mom and Dad savored those two long years together despite the struggles and steady decline in her health. Their determined example of acceptance through faith was more than inspirational it was life-changing. Each of us, her children, our children, her friends and all of the many others who made their way into their lives those last two years were blessed through their steady faith, bold courage, and simple hope in accepting God's plan for their lives. Their devotion to one another was beautiful and convicting to watch. In the midst of this terrible struggle for life they carried themselves with dignity as a patient example to us all. Through the valley their light shone brightly.

When my Mom was in her last few months and still able to really influence us in a proactive manner she called me one day to talk about "some questions". The first thing she asked was whether or not I would speak at her memorial - that was a daunting challenge to say the least. The next question was even bigger, "Why am I being punished?" I left hospice that day confused and worried that I could not fill those shoes or even begin to answer her concerns. But God is great, and it was at about that time that he had first opened my heart and mind to his word. We shared many precious visits together, a son and his mother, considering her question, her worries, and her final reality that dying was imminent. Looking back I think that what she meant by punishment was not as retribution for sin, but as a kind of social or relational penalty.

Her fear that a lifetime of smoking, what many would perceive as selfish behavior, was being drawn out for public display by an angry Father. But, it was not this punishment from God that worried her so much as it was the public humiliation. She had accepted mortality. She was personally at ease with her cancer and understood it to be the result of a risk she had born with open eyes. I believe what she considered her actual punishment was that all would know. There was no hiding the fact, that some among us would smugly be saying, "I told you so", and she had no defense, no graceful options. She was afraid, not of death, but of its impersonal, irrevocable finality. She did not want to die as the woman with lung cancer. She wanted to die as a lady of awesome faith and dedication to family. She sincerely wanted to present God with the fruit of her faith, not of sin. As an intensely private person her entire life she considered these conditions a punishment and it didn't equate to a loving God. My awkward reassurances that God does not punish his children, but that he allows trials into our lives to bring us closer to him through endurance and reliance were never really the issue, she already got that. It was the stigma of lung cancer that was the problem. She was truly remorseful of her cancer and sought faithfully to make some final compensation for it. It was God's word that would lead me to the answer she really sought.

How often, how many times a day do I catch myself trying to divine the Father's motives, his perfect plan for my life? Each and every time two things are patiently made clear. I can never anticipate God, and God's plan is always far greater and more beautiful than I could ever have created for myself. So why do I, why do any of us continually fall for the notion that we know best, that we are in full control? The fact that we are physical beings in a physical world attempting to submit to spiritual direction in a spiritual world is just the beginning of it. The urgency of time, the clamor of five selfish senses, and the disparate examples of others serve only to drown out and override most of the humble inclinations our souls impart.

We live an intensely physical existence in a barely discernible spiritual world our reflexes and defenses are set for immediate threats and immediate rewards, not the whispers of faith. It seems that even when we manage to silence the world just long enough to be still, that our resolve is immediately onset by the inevitable doubts and confusion. Eventually, faith becomes not just a static quality, an asset that is predictably managed, but rather, a dynamic force, changing and growing in endurance as we face the trials that define and mold our lives. It seems it takes a collaborative willingness through faith on our part, that God can then direct through his word, to achieve the miracles we dare to dream of.

This year my Dad's brother Ed passed away after a long illness. His memorial service was in Texas and my Dad's health prevented him from being there so I went in his place. I wanted to be able to give Dad a firsthand account and also offer Ed's family some support. It was a simple service, humble, unpretentious, an honest reflection of his faith. At the end of the service the pastor explained that Ed had made a special request, actually his only request, that there might be an offer to receive salvation for anyone present that was ready and willing. At the time I thought it a little unusual for a memorial service, but the more I considered it the more sense it made, especially with a man like my uncle Ed who was such a strong believer and servant throughout his life. Later that day as I was leaving for the airport, my cousin Charles offered to walk out to the car. We were making our goodbyes when he surprised me by saying that he was not saved, that he was bitter from several traumas in his life, especially the sudden death of his young daughter. He admitted that he was trying but that he just couldn't see the way. The sadness in his voice was minor compared to the burden in his eyes. He was struggling and wanted so badly to believe, to be assured that his terrible circumstances had not been needless but had meaning and hope, that there was more to life than suffering and death.

It was a powerful moment for me when the realization sank in that Ed had used his last moments on Earth to reach out and offer one last time to his struggling son the gift of the gospel. It was difficult to talk because the majesty of the moment was so overwhelming. God's hands were all over this day. Charles was so close and yet still so far away and his father was lovingly committing this day not to himself but to his son. All I could manage was to try to share the beauty of the truth and pray that time and God's healing spirit would do the rest. I told him about my experience with Mom's death and the question we had struggled with her last few weeks, about the timeliness of God's word in my life and then I told him about the rich man.

The rich man is an old friend of mine. By that I mean I have visited his story in Luke many, many times. He has a lot to say and he has been condemned to repeat it for two thousand years. The really sad part is that he will be saying it for eternity. He is known by no other name than the rich man, which is a description of his lecherous life and worldly pride. We know he buried himself in splendor, that any charity he practiced was doled out as some meager legalistic atonement, and that he came to know the gospel far too late. In his defense we also know he had a family and that he cared for them in his own small way. My brother Scott introduced me to him about six years ago. It was his humble way of telling me I needed help, it was also the day that my heart began to open to God's word. The rich man and Lazarus are two of God's most earnest spokesmen and they spoke directly to my heart.

There are many important messages in this story, but as a father there are two that stand out most. The first is that we are not placed on this earth just to luxuriate in all it has to offer. Yes, we should enjoy and be awestruck by every possible wonder, that can be discovered, but we shouldn't be fooled into thinking they are free without responsibility, that they exist just for exploitation. We are placed on this earth to make one decision and one decision only, and God's gift of this awesome world is his way of prefacing what is to come. The physical glory here is just a token of what he promises for heaven. To settle for the worldly today is to settle far short of the promise our Father has made for tomorrow and forever.

The second message is that my example as a father will be learned and lived by others. So often, people are fooled into thinking that their decision for faith is solely a private matter, that what they decide is no one else's business and it should not be used to encourage or discourage others. This parable specifically reminds us that our actions are indeed a critical model that will shape and define those who follow us, those who look up to us. We cannot take this responsibility lightly or privately, we must lead and in order to do so we must be properly equipped. The rich man discovers much too late the awful fate his materialism has earned, it is even too late to warn those whom he respected and admired in life. One wonders what their reaction to him will be when they too find themselves on the wrong shore of eternity. As parents, we will exhaust our resources and ourselves, providing for the physical wellbeing of our children. How can it be possible that we would not want or strive for the same development in their faith life? Faced with the horrible reality presented by the rich man I was forced to consider more than just myself and more than just what I could see, hear, feel, smell and taste in the world around me. I was patiently, persuasively and finally led into God's loving arms. I prayed that Charles too might be moved by the rich man and welcomed by Christ.

One of the miracles of God's word is that even though it was written for all people, it can and should be read as a private, loving, personal conversation. It is alive and powerful, it is true, it teaches and corrects us, it opens our understanding to God's will, it leads us to Christ, it endures forever, it is sweeter than honey, and it is so much more. It was God's word that I went to in looking for some way to help Mom face her worries, it was the word that began to reassure me and lead me to peace, and it was the word that Ed was trusting would save his son from the prison his pain had placed him in. Another of the many miracles of the word is that once you begin to consider it, to let its messages fill your heart, it changes you from the inside out. It fills the voids you are aware of and it finds those you never knew you had.

This cooperative effort between the reader and the word is in essence a partnership. God does his best work through partnerships, and the incredible irony of it is that we often never know what has transpired until much later. Mom's questions, Ed's memorial request, the warning of the rich man were all a part of one simple, life-changing, life-saving plan that drew each of us closer to him. I am comforted today knowing that Mom had sensed all along that I had been rebellious and that she was "partnering" with God to allow him to work in my heart by addressing her questions. I also believe that my uncle Ed was using the most solemn day of his life to share the greatest gift of his life with the people he loved the most by partnering with God to place peace in Charles's heart. I am grateful to have met the rich man when I did, I thank him for his message, and I thank God for his word and the opportunity to share this story.

"I can never escape from your Spirit! I can never get away from your presence! If I go up to Heaven you are there; if I go down to the grave you are there."
                              Psalm 139:7-8

CHAPTER 10

"To Know Is Forever"

"That is why I am suffering here in prison. But I am not ashamed of it, for I know the One in whom I believe, and I am persuaded that he is able to guard what I have entrusted to him until the day of his return."
2 Timothy 1:12

Paul was nearing the end of his life. He was imprisoned and almost forgotten by those to whom he had devoted so much of his ministry when he wrote this second letter to Timothy, his son in the faith. It was a letter of encouragement with specific instructions for carrying on the work that they had begun together. It also emphasized the essentials that Paul knew were crucial for the growth, not only of the church, but each individual in it. He knew too well the dangers of false doctrine and misplaced faith, of the stresses of the world, of hopelessness and lost faith, of material problems designed to impede spiritual solutions. For these reasons he encouraged Timothy to "fan into flames the spiritual gift God had given him" when he first believed, to put into action the grace he had received. As he sat alone, separated from his friends and fellow believers, Paul was led to ponder and appreciate the essence of what it truly means to know the Savior.

Through his optimistic style Paul was both coach and teacher in reminding and strengthening

Timothy in the foundational tenets of his relationship with God. Perhaps the most important advice that can be found in this letter is that addressing the divide between believing in God and knowing God, or rather, the spiritual progression that one must complete in establishing an eternal relationship in salvation.

To believe is to have faith in the truth of the Good News, to have earnestly sought Him out. To know is to have received God's grace, to become one of his children, to have been reborn. To believe is to have heard and willingly answered the knock on the door; to know is to have opened it and shared a meal. In making this crucial distinction Paul was reminding Timothy of the central, undeniable, non-negotiable first step that any believer must make in his or her walk with God.
We cannot know God without first having faith, without having first believed in Him and wholeheartedly embraced the Good News. It is only after faith opens our heart that God's grace can enter in and initiate the miracle of salvation. To know is the eternal state we arrive at from having accepted and believed beforehand. Paul was urging Timothy to "fan" his faith, to convert it from belief to knowledge. Scripture tells us that we cannot know God without first believing in Him, "without faith it is impossible to please God, because anyone who comes to him must believe that he exists and that he rewards those who earnestly seek him". But Scripture also warns that we can believe there is a God and yet fail to know Him, "You say you have faith, for you believe that

there is one God. Good for you! Even the demons believe this, and they tremble in terror".

    In his final days Paul was providing an earnest invitation for his students to be persuaded by, to believe in, and then to know without shame the God of his forefathers and the only God of salvation. In typical workmanlike fashion he illustrated this distinction between knowing and believing, a distinction that he considered to be so crucial to the validity and strength and endurance of one's life in faith. Leaving nothing to chance, he reminded Timothy to expect rejection, false prophesy, and persecution. He insisted that constancy and perseverance should be his focus. He was warned against being entangled in the affairs of this world, and instructed that if believers are to partake of the fruit we must first be willing to run the race, and run it faithfully.

    Paul also viewed faith as a living principle, which requires constant exercise and devotion in order to sustain it. To him it was not enough just to believe the Gospel, instead, he determined that it must be loved and that its truthfulness in our lives be embraced and lived out through us. Again and again he challenged Timothy not to be ashamed to suffer for the Gospel, that it was intended to sanctify and define his life. His frank advice was not to let fear or timidity prevent him from sharing and teaching the Gospel, that ultimately carrying God's word to his people would bear him out and deliver him the crown of righteousness as a prize for all "who eagerly look forward to the day of Christ's return".

Through this letter to Timothy, Paul's concept of belief can be seen as an understanding, and the state of knowing as putting that belief into action, reaffirming it, consolidating it and embedding it into our very souls. It was this active, daily, moment-by-moment commitment to one's belief that Paul was urging Timothy to demonstrate and encourage in all of his disciples. Like James, Paul was warning that faith without action was dead and useless. Paul boldly declared, "If we die with him, we will also live with him. If we endure hardship, we will reign with him. If we deny him, he will deny us. If we are unfaithful, he remains faithful, for he cannot deny who he is".

So how do we know God, how do we get past simple acknowledgement and reach true enlightenment? First, we must believe and welcome the Good News unconditionally into our hearts. The Good News must enter us and change us. We must be reborn. Christ put it this way, *"Unless you are born again, you cannot see the kingdom of God".* We must be inspired by it and through it. We indwell in it and it, in turn, indwells us. Faith in God comes from hearing the Good News, and the gospel is the power of God for salvation. It is heard, pondered and believed. Everyone who calls on the Name of the Lord will be saved. Scripture promises that there is salvation in no one else.

Second, we must not be ashamed, but obligated and eager. We must put aside the past, the condemnations, and the failed self-righteous view of ourselves and embrace the glory of today and tomorrow. John Piper explains it this way, "the gospel brings out shaming behavior in those who will not believe it and it gives freedom from shame for those who do". Therefore, we know through conviction where we stand. We declare our faith and we claim God's grace. The reward for trusting God is the salvation of our souls. God saves us by His grace, when we first believed. It is a free gift. And lastly, through this grace God gives us a heart to know Him. To believe is for today, to know is forever.

"And it is impossible to please God without faith. Anyone who wants to come to him must believe that God exists and that he rewards those who sincerely seek him."
Hebrews 11:6

CHAPTER 11

"What Is Right?"

"The Lord has told you what is good, and this is what he requires of you; to do what is right, to love mercy, and to walk humbly with your God."
                                            Micah 6:8

    It's interesting how we live out our lives under the umbrella of a multitude of conventional standards, from social to personal to occupational to ethical, and yet we never really question the validity or practical authority they represent. Passively we accept standards that declare rightness without the slightest scrutiny and confer compliance without regard to precedent. Society demands a certain degree of conformity and, through our haphazard human process of trial and error a generally accepted barometer has evolved from which we can judge the "rightness" of just about any activity you care to name. As a result, both the idea and the habit of submitting to standardization is not alien to human nature. In fact, under almost all circumstances it is the relative security that such standards represent which serves to reinforce the universal conviction many people hold, that since man can successfully establish them then why should he ever defer to another authority, especially to God.
    In other words, many skeptics would say, "We're doing just fine without you, so why subject ourselves to the auspices of some ancient rules

that we know little about?" But is man really better off? Is he really secure in moral relativism? Does right exist legitimately in relative terms? Can man independently and merely through his frail, human efforts determine what is right?

When we first accept the premise of relative standards, the necessary dilemma, which follows is the reconciliation of any actions, which might arise from them. If what was right today is not right tomorrow, then what is right, and if it is right for you does it necessarily have to be right for me? Does man actually profit from a measure, which has no demonstrable beginning or end? Relative standards are just that, they are relative. They have no intrinsic authority from which to gauge confidence. So, the difficulty with adherence to a relative standard for morality finally boils down to the problem of inconsistency. A standard with no fixed foundation is no standard at all. It is merely a whim - an incidental, untested, unfaithful, inefficient, capricious guess - definitely not the stock from which successful lives and civilizations generally arise. In fact, without a defined standard from which to measure does the concept of right ever have any meaning at all?

Regrettably, the secular argument for any relative standard, which attempts to define right fails in the final analysis, and defaults to man's traditional expedient strategy, which is always to create a new one, a new right. This eventually fails as well. Man's unceasing search for a self-reliant standard, rather than focusing in on the one, unchangeable, eternal source, invariably leads us further and further from the gold standard which has always been immediately available, wasting a lot of time and precious human resources in the process.

The Roman emperor Marcus Aurelius said,

"Live a good life. If there are gods and they are just, then they will not care how devout you have been, but will welcome you based on the virtues you have lived by. If there are gods, but unjust, then you should not want to worship them. If there are no gods, then you will be gone, but will have lived a noble life that will live on in the memories of your loved ones".

In other words, "Do what you think is right or at least what people say is right, and no matter what the circumstances after death at least your buddies will hoist a toast or two". Marcus Aurelius was a Stoic. He lived an austere, temperate, moral life, which reflected his philosophical reverence for the value of all life, of one's work, and even in Roman times, of basic human rights. On the surface many people would find his advice both reassuring and practical. In a word, they would find it right. So, what objections should we have with this simple advice, and I guess more importantly, what is it about what he says that is just not right?

In a sense Marcus Aurelius was a man ahead of his time. He was an advocate for moral relativity long before the concept was ever articulated. In his defense, he believed in personal responsibility, in the integrity of self, and even in a deity of some type. On the surface he was a popular ruler and his influence was for the most part positive, but if you were an early Christian it was demoralizing. As an emperor he was a zealous persecutor of Christians and sadly it was his stoicism that fueled that fire.

Not surprisingly, a closer look at this philosophy reveals the source of his hatred for the Christian God as well as his ambivalence towards social structure. At the heart of the Stoic philosophy lays a god, but not the God of Christ, it is the god of self, of self-reliance and of self-determination. The Stoic takes pride in being a burden to no one, at helping others, at social equality and fiscal frugality - all laudable qualities to be sure. But, the god of the Stoic could not and would not accept the total submission and faith required of the God of the Christians, and the full force of Aurelius' imperial might was directed against it. For Marcus Aurelius it was simple, a war between the invincible god of man and the invisible God of the Christian. Like many before him and countless many after, he was so close yet so far away. Did he really believe, deep down inside, that goodness bought godliness, and if he did, did he really live it out? How does a great man with such talent and promise lose sight, or perhaps never have it, of the eternal truth of the God of Christ? Simple, it is never knowing what is right. And how do we fail to know right? Simple, in relative terms it is always changing, it is never the "right" right.

As material beings we must have help to see right. Jesus taught us that the eye is a lamp that provides light for the body. When our eye is good, our whole body is filled with light. But when it is bad, our body is filled with darkness. The word of God brings light to everyone and the good news is that Scripture teaches us what is true and what is wrong in our lives. It corrects us when we are wrong and teaches us to do what is right. In other words, right becomes a relationship, our relationship with God through Christ through his word. And because it is only through faith in Christ that we are made righteous in God's eyes, right becomes the reflection of our faith.

Through faith, Christ opens our hearts to right and then he helps us walk by that faith rather than sight. It doesn't mean that faith is blind, on the contrary, it means faith is another way of seeing, not relative to the material world around us. Faith "sees" that God exists and that his promises are more reliable than our own natural instincts. Faith trusts God's promises over the world's perceptions which means that in order for Christians to see correctly we must depend implicitly on the "precious and very great promises of God", his Scriptures. Our great faith in Christ makes us right with God through his living word, and that is what is right.

"This Good News tells us how God makes us right in his sight. This is accomplished from start to finish by faith."
Romans 1:17

CHAPTER 12

"If I Have Faltered More Or Less"

"So I say, let the Holy Spirit guide your lives. Then you won't be doing what your sinful nature craves."
Galatians 5:16

One day some people were gathered with Jesus and they challenged him by comparing his disciples to those of other religious leaders. They noted that the disciples of John the Baptist, as well as those of the Pharisees fasted and prayed regularly. A lifestyle, which was in stark contrast to that seen in his followers who were "always eating and drinking". The implication being that Christ's followers were not serious enough, or sacrificially conformed enough in their attitudes to be legitimate disciples, that their theology was just too joyous to be worth the pursuit. His response to their question was both direct and prophetic. *"Do wedding guests fast while celebrating with the groom? Of course not, but someday the groom will be taken away from them, and then they will fast."* He gave them this illustration: "No one tears a piece of cloth from a new garment and uses it to patch an old garment. For then the new garment would be ruined, and the new patch wouldn't even match the old garment. And no one puts new wine into old wineskins. For the new wine would burst the wineskins, spilling the wine and ruining the skins. New wine must be stored in new wineskins.

But no one who drinks the old wine seems to want the new wine. 'The old is just fine' they say."

This question of propriety, of behavioral correctness is one we can struggle with every day. But more important is not so much our behavior, but the attitude, the belief that shapes it. Christ was telling his detractors that their rote behavior, their rigid adherence to Mosaic Law, their "showy" rejection of God's glorious invitation was in fact just proof of their blind selfishness. "The old is just fine", they said. They were unwilling to step out of the safety of good deeds, confessions of sin and redemption through sacrificial offering. They were more willing to suffer finite privation today than to consider infinite separation tomorrow. But Christ warned them, *"Someday the groom will be taken away from them, and then they will fast."* By promising that there would come a day when God would no longer accept repentance and that eternal remorse would begin, he was begging them to disregard their legalism, their self-righteousness, their devotion to institutional propitiation, and to hear the truth of the gospel.

These words from Christ, as recorded by Luke and later expanded on by Paul, teach us two essential points about living the Christian life. The first is that we must live in the constant hope of our salvation through the presence and direction of the Holy Spirit. And secondly, that in order for our salvation to be complete we must first die in our "old skins" and be born again in new ones.

"The Celestial Surgeon" a sonnet by Robert Louis Stevenson is one author's plea perhaps, about the daily struggle each of us is faced with in denying the old self while seeking and inviting the new one in. Stevenson admits his "faltering", his unmoving attitude, his "sullen heart" and begs God to "stab my spirit broad awake" with some "pointed pleasure". And if that fails, if he is too stubborn or obdurate, that "before that spirit die", to chose instead a "piercing pain, a killing sin" to bring him to his senses. In other words, just like the disciples of John the Baptist and the Pharisees before him, Stevenson's faith was being overwhelmed by rote and ritual, when what he really sought was to eat and drink with Christ. He is begging his celestial surgeon to pierce him with a soul-awakening worldly miracle or, if that failed, to attempt a physically painful one, and to do it before it was too late. This is a poem about remorse, about repentance, and finally about redemption. It admits to the fruitless life of a self-centered man, of the denial of God's daily presence around him, and hopefully of his final realization that only God can save him.

The Celestial Surgeon

"If I have faltered more or less
In my great task of happiness;
If I have moved among my race
And shown no glorious morning face;
If beams from happy human eyes
Have moved me not; if morning skies
Books, and my food, and summer rain

Knocked on my sullen heart in vain:
Lord, thy most pointed pleasure take
And stab my spirit broad awake;
Or, Lord, if too obdurate I,
Choose thou, before that spirit die,
A piercing pain, a killing sin,
And to my dead heart run them in!"
R. L. Stevenson

As I write this essay today I am sitting quite comfortably on a lofty veranda overlooking the beautiful azure Caribbean, sunlight is dancing on a rippled sea and trade wind gusts rattle the palms and toss butterflies from one glorious coloration to another. It should be impossible not to see God's work in all of this splendor, to hear it on the wind, to feel it on the skin, but its not, Christ knew it and I feel it just like those people who first posed the question. For a moment today, more moments than I dare to admit, I too was busied in my self, focused on my immediate doubts and not on my future promise. Like me, they were not curious so much about the actual behavior of Christ's followers as they were about what it was that was so crucial about his message. What did Christ have to offer that could be so profound as to lead his believers out of their comfort zone, their traditional safe havens, their old selves and without the recourse of a "patch", to be irrevocably committed.

The answer is in understanding that the "old skin" cannot be patched, it cannot contain the new, and it is not "just fine". Paul advises us to let the Holy Spirit guide our lives. Then we won't be doing what our sinful nature craves. That when we are directed by the Spirit we are not under obligation to the Law of Moses, and most importantly of all, that the Spirit produces in our lives love, joy, peace, patience, kindness, goodness, faithfulness, gentleness and self-control. Those who belong to Christ Jesus have nailed the passions and desires of their sinful nature to his cross and crucified them there. What Christ offered his followers was true salvation and its proof was in his Spirit. What the people saw was the fruit, the joy that no man could take away, the joy of the presence of God. What the people really needed to be seeking was not so much what Christ's disciples had. What they really needed to seek was what Stevenson asked for, for God's intervention in their lives, any way they could get it, and in any form that He chose.

"They know the truth about God because he has made it obvious to them. For ever since the world was created, people have seen the earth and sky. Through everything God made, they can clearly see his invisible qualities, his eternal power and divine nature. So they have no excuse for not knowing God."
Romans 1:19-20

CHAPTER 13

"Don't Count On It"

"Satan rose up against Israel and caused David to take a census of the people of Israel."
                              1 Chronicles 21:1

How many times have you heard, "Don't count your chickens before they hatch", and thought, "Yeah, yeah, I hear you, but this one's in the bag, you guys might not be able to figure things out, but I sure can." It's so ingrained in most of us that this stale old saying really has no bite; it's irrelevant in the contemporary world. Planning, and especially focused, purposeful, considered planning has become anathema to the fast-paced, spontaneous digital world of nonchalance and uncommitted resignation that seem to reflect our modern attitudes. Real men, we're told, don't have to plan because the world will submit anyway. So this story of King David being punished for actually daring to plan would seem to be no big deal considering that most of us don't want the worry anyway.

How is it that taking a census, getting a head count of all his subjects, could be such a big deal? You would certainly think that any effort to manage and improve the efficiency of his kingdom would have been met with approval, or at the very least a measured diffidence, not the catastrophic reaction that followed. So, what specifically about looking to the future, about having the audacity to plan, was it that compromised David's intentions?

At first glance it appears he was just exercising his royal privilege, his duties as a king. But, when we dig deeper we discover that this census was not undertaken in complete innocence, it was not without it's worldly influences. As it turns out David was not acting on the Lord's behalf, he was acting on his own. His motives were not spiritually honest they were downright prideful and rebellious. David was after his own glory. He was plotting his own destiny.

In ancient times there were two legitimate reasons that a census might be ordered, for the purposes of redemption as directed by God, and for military planning as directed by the King. It was for this second application that David had ordered his survey. It was the Spring of the year, "when kings normally go to war", and having missed the siege of Rabbah, David was eager and willing to cut a few corners to mix it up, to sate his ego. But, in order to get things going he needed knowledge, he needed to know the strength of his army. He had just added the crown of the king of the Ammonites to his collection and he was narrowly focused on getting more. One new hat was simply not good enough. God had given him victory over his enemies, but David was not satisfied, he was giddy for more. His seeming invincibility and overwhelming firepower had convinced him of self-righteousness, of destiny. He was counting his next victory, wearing his next crown, making his next great proclamation without any direction from God. The voice of reason that was winning his ear unfortunately though was not that of God, but the stealthy voice of Satan and the result was catastrophic.

So how do we get there, how do we begin in grace and wind up in tragedy? How do things start out so well, just to end with loss? Scripture tells us, *"Don't brag about tomorrow, since you don't know what the day will bring."* The skeptic might say, "Okay, so laissez faire is cool after all, I'm all about indecision, relativity reigns!" But that's not what this message is really about. The Bible says, "You don't know." So the real question is, who does know, and how do I get plugged in, how do I get to know?

David's problem was that he listened to the wrong voice. Satan led him through pride. He was caught up in his successes and "planning on" the future not "praying for" it. He was counting on successes without considering their cost, and even worse, not considering their source. His total confidence in himself reflected a lack of confidence in God, and the result was a rejection, not only of the advice of others, but of God's intentions as well. It was this rejection of God's direction in his life that led to the eventual calamity that befell him. David's problems were subtle, but they bear careful consideration. Scripture tells us the "plan" to order a census was not his but was planted by the devil.

I can't count the number of times I have been excited by a "great idea" just to realize in time and through God's mercy, that it was nothing but another bad idea, hidden behind a brand new face. If the revelation is not God-inspired, it is likely devil-inspired and therefore, never in your best interests. Even after David was counseled by his trusted advisers. He ignored them and pushed on. It was pride that blinded him and pride that left him no apparent options. It was also pride that curried his self-reliance and left him reluctant to place his confidence in God's leadership. Once outside the protective sphere of godly direction, he was basically rudderless and ineffective as a leader. Ultimately he was isolated and impotent and the choices that he faced grew not surprisingly from bad to worse.

How many times have you found yourself in this corner? The sad truth is, most of us happily strut into this spot and, once there, blame anything and everyone else other than ourselves for the result. David was no different and the Bible says that seventy thousand people lost their lives as a consequence.

James put it this way when he wrote, "Look here, you who say, today or tomorrow we are going to a certain town and will stay there a year, we will do business there and make a profit! How do you know what your life will be like tomorrow? Your life is like the morning fog, it's here a little while and then it's gone. What you ought to say is, if the Lord wants us to, we will live and do this or that. Otherwise you are boasting about your plans, and all such boasting is evil." In so many words James is cautioning us not to be like David, led by the wrong spirit, the spirit of the world, but to seek

God's direction in all things. The message that really begs to be seen through this story of David is that decision-making should always reflect the Lord's intentions, not ours. It is not enough just to remain unmoved, frozen in lassitude, or to take matters indiscriminately and without spiritual reflection into our own hands. Paul wrote, "Pray about everything. Tell God what you need and thank him for all he has done. Then you will experience God's peace, which exceeds anything we can understand. His peace will guard your hearts and minds as you live in Jesus Christ." Paul is saying that decisions are not really ours. At the end of the day we should be much more focused on carrying out orders than plotting to enact them. We shouldn't worry about counting our chickens, because they are not ours to count, rather we should be tending them. And in order to be a good tender we must first submit our will to His, we must turn and follow his laws. And then we will know.

"Remember, it is a sin to know what you ought to do, and then not do it."
James 4:17

CHAPTER 14

"The Teacher's Dream"

"And the Lord said to Paul one night in a vision, "Do not be afraid, but go on speaking and do not be silent".
Acts 18:9–11

I had a dream last night. I was teaching at the dental school and was in a classroom with a group of students discussing a rare anesthetic complication known as malignant hyperthermia. As a part-time teacher I was playing an adjunct role and was actually just standing there as the full-time professor led the formal discussion. Her talk was basically a compendium of current available evidence-based knowledge that medicine has concerning MH and the students were rapid-fire responding to all the prompts she interjected into the lecture. As an on-looker, not so equipped with all the ivory tower details, I felt more than a little out of place and when I was finally asked a question by one of the students my anecdote-based response was essentially dismissed by the professor and she went on as though my contribution was completely inadequate.

Later, as I left the building to return home at the end of a long day of contributing very little, I was confronted in the poorly lit parking lot by three thugs intent on robbing me, or worse. When I objected to their threats, the leader said, "Shut up". As the dream meandered I remember escaping through another office building where I saw a janitor who saved me from my pursuers. He ushered me safely back to the dental school building where I found myself waiting to talk to the Chairman of the department, but met a student instead. We were having an amazing discussion as I recall and as the dream ended I found myself talking to myself rebutting the professor's purely theoretical stance on her advice regarding the identification and treatment of MH. I argued that my practical side of the equation was much more applicable and important than the purely empirical one she had insisted upon, and I regretted not having had the opportunity to share it with all the other students who were completely dazzled by her educational and technological charm.

When I awoke it dawned on me that what this dream was really all about was faith. Defending the faith. Obligingly. Eagerly. Unashamedly. Yes, there are any number of inarguable stances that a skeptic can take that we as believers have no response for simply because the argument is couched in terms that allow no admittance to matters of faith. The realm of the skeptic is strictly the realm of rational proof, the realm of statistics and empirical standards, a digital, all-or-none world of black or white with no tolerance to grey.

I was never expected to speak authoritatively to the students simply because I was unable to convey my beliefs and experiences in the language in which they spoke. My world of experience leading to faith cannot be calibrated or double blind tested, its just one man's word. I was muted from the get go and unfortunately the student's resultant perception was completely stilted. Yes, they knew the scientific argument inside and out, but only to the point where that argument ends with the "latest" evidence from the "most recent" and "trending" savants of their field. What they were never allowed to consider was my testimony of what actually happens on the ground, in real life, in the living breathing zone where quantum theory breaks down and real time decisions result in reality, not some ideal that seems always to be just on the horizon. What I really wanted to tell them all along was that experience begins where the horizon ends, that experience through faith does not replace or refute hard science, rather it completes it. Faith takes it where it could never go by itself. Experience through faith takes the believer beyond the horizon.

And as I write this today, some twelve hours after awaking, it occurs to me that a horizon is just that, its an endpoint on your material timeline, but you can never reach it physically because the closer you move towards it the further it moves away, unless of course, you change your vantage. If I remain bound to the material world, I am fated like Sisyphus to a never-ending work, a relative horizon that has no hope of attainment. In order to reach the horizon you must make a huge leap. You must skip over the material world to have access to the spiritual. The material horizon is comparable to the empty spot in a person's heart, which longs for meaning. They will exhaust all means available to force the material world into a spiritual hole and never fill it, because they can never reach the bottom. The material world is by definition finite and, mercifully, it can only go so far. Those of us who are truly blessed discover that law long before the pain of emptiness becomes unbearable. The rest sadly must hit bottom. What I remember most on awakening this morning was trying desperately to speak the student's language, to convince them of the finite nature of the world, and feeling so helpless until my savior arrived.

"But sanctify Christ as Lord in your hearts, always being ready to make a defense to everyone who asks you to give an account for the hope that is in you, yet with gentleness and reverence".
   1Peter 3:15

Addendum:

   The British poet, T.S. Eliot wrote in his poem, "Little Gidding", a stanza that has impacted my thinking for some time. In just four short lines he managed to articulate perfectly what it means to know something for the first time, and his very subtle point is that in order to truly know something it must first be sought out, then discovered for what it is, and only then known for the first time. How else can I identify something if I have never missed it, if I have never acknowledged its absence? Isn't that so true for coming to faith? We must explore, we must discover and only then can we actually know it for what it is? How else can one decide without first "arriving where they started"?

> *"We shall not cease from exploration*
> *And the end of all our exploring*
> *Will be to arrive where we started*
> *And know the place for the first time."*
> T. S. Eliot, "Little Gidding"

Henry David Thoreau said much the same thing, just a little less poetically, but with the added emphasis that we must be committed to our search if we are ever to discover what we seek.

> *"Many an object is not seen, though it falls within the range of our visual ray, because it does not come within the range of our intellectual ray, i.e. we are not looking for it. So, in the largest sense, we find only the world we look for."*
> H. Thoreau, 2 July 1857

Khalil Gibran carried these observations one step further in reminding us that although others may do the leading, each of us must independently and intentionally seek our own understanding and our own faith.

> *"No man can reveal to you aught but that which already lies half asleep in the dawning of your knowledge. The teacher who walks in the shadow of the temple, among his followers, gives not of his wisdom but rather of his faith and his lovingness. If he is indeed wise he does not bid you enter the house of his wisdom, but rather leads you to the threshold of your own mind. The astronomer may speak to you of his*

understanding of space, but he cannot give you his understanding. The musician may sing to you of the rhythm, which is in all space, but he cannot give you the ear, which arrests the rhythm nor the voice that echoes it. And he who is versed in the science of numbers can tell of the regions of weight and measure, but he cannot conduct you thither. For the vision of one man lends not its wings to another man. And even as each one of you stands alone in God's knowledge, so must each one of you be alone in his knowledge of God and in his understanding of the earth."

K. Gibran, "The Prophet"

CHAPTER 15

"Obedience Is Better Than Sacrifice"

"What is more pleasing to the Lord, your burnt offerings and sacrifices or your obedience to his voice? Listen! Obedience is better than sacrifice, and submission is better than offering the fat of rams".
1Samuel 15:22

King Saul was instructed by God to carry out a specific task, to eradicate a certain nation including all of its people and property, but in the process of carrying out those orders he decided on his own to spare the opposing king and some of his choice livestock to present as a pleasing sacrifice to God. Much to Saul's surprise this "sacrifice" was rejected outright, and to make matters even worse he was overthrown as king of Israel. Scripture records his indignation and desperate pleading as he attempted to rationalize his version of disobedience compensated in sacrifice. Saul honestly valued his self-righteous wisdom over the will of God right up to the very moment he was finally and irrevocably overthrown. It's a sad ending to a powerful story of a man not unlike many of us who set out with all good intentions but ultimately failed because he thought he knew better, he trusted his material instincts over his spiritual voice and he chose sacrifice over obedience.

Sacrifice or obedience, it's a decision that we face every day, do I comply with a specific request that has been made of me, or do I pursue the more convenient or satisfying alternative, one that in and of itself might require some extra effort, some weighted cost? Saul was clearly instructed on what to do and yet, in his "I know better" mode, made a decision, which served his personal and political aspirations over those of God. He yielded to pressure from those whom he was charged to lead, and rather than carry out specific instructions to the contrary, he managed to unravel and destroy all of the achievements that had measured his life up to that point. Jesus explained it this way, *"No one can serve two masters. Either you will hate the one and love the other, or you will be devoted to the one and despise the other. You cannot serve both God and money"*. So how do we serve both God and man without being destroyed in the fray? How do we deserve such an unfair choice? How do seemingly good intentions manage to achieve the exact opposite? Even more to the point, what is it about sacrifice that attracts disobedience, how am I led to quantify, much less justify the price of obedience?

One day a young man came to Jesus and asked him, "Good teacher, what must I do to inherit eternal life?" The Bible tells us he was a teacher himself and a man of considerable affluence, a leader. He also considered himself to be righteous by Jewish law and this question for Christ may have been as much a reflection of pride as it was an honest inquiry. It was not uncommon for Jewish scholars to test Christ's knowledge and interpretation of scripture, but Jesus did not hesitate and responded immediately with three direct truths. First, he reminded the young man that only God is truly good, that no one is capable of ever being sinless on his own effort. No matter his circumstances be they great or small, goodness cannot be purchased. More to the point, he asserted that there is no way to eternal life except through God. Next, with that foundation firmly established he declared that even if one were to follow all of God's commandments one's efforts would still be inadequate when they are carried out for selfish purposes. In other words, if a man's motivation for obedience is self-serving, no matter how sacrificial or altruistic, it is still fruitless. And just as in Saul's case, to make matters worse, it is rebellious and does not please God. Lastly, Matthew records that with genuine love Jesus then challenged the young man to abandon his worldly pursuits and to follow him, to obey without question or regret. It was on this final point that the young man blinked. He was willing to sacrifice but he was unwilling to obey. Scripture tells us matter-of-factly that he went away sad for he had many possessions. Sacrifice thus becomes love of this world, obedience becomes love of God, and in these terms obedience is always better than sacrifice.

The apostle Paul declared in his letter to God's church in Corinth that three things last forever - faith, hope and love - and the greatest of these is love. Love enforces our faith and empowers our hope. Love also assures their fulfillment because the more we bring love into our lives the more our faith and hope will grow, both in ourselves and in the lives of those we live for. Paul pointed right to the heart of this paradox between obedience and sacrifice by examining it in terms of love, specifically, the love of God versus the love of self.

"If I speak in the tongues of men and of angels, but have not love, I am only a resounding gong or a clanging cymbal. If I have the gift of prophecy and can fathom all mysteries and all knowledge, and if I have a faith that can move mountains, but have not love, I am nothing. If I give all I possess to the poor and surrender my body to the flames, but have not love, I gain nothing".
1Cor 13:1-3

His observation sheds a sobering light on our dilemma. At first, it would appear to be a contradiction when Paul says that if he gives all that he possesses to the poor and he surrenders his body to the flames, but does not have love, he gains nothing. How do I gain nothing when I have sacrificed all that I have? What is so striking about this statement is the thought of how Paul could possibly give away all that he has to the poor without love. How could he willingly suffer deprivation or torture or worse without love? On the surface it is hard to imagine any person eager to accept such responsibility without an honest, legitimate reason. You would expect to enjoy incredible, overwhelming, unconditional love first before any of these things could ever be possible, what else could suffice?

But sadly, Paul worries that it is, in fact, possible to do much and it is possible to suffer much, and yet not have love, or at least not have love other than of oneself. Next he warns us that whatever we have done or sacrificed without godly love means nothing. In the words of Isaiah, we can proudly display all our righteous deeds, but at the end of the day, they are like filthy rags, because they are born from self-love, not godly love. For most of us this is hard to accept because scripture tells us that when we sacrifice to God He is pleased. But the point that Samuel and Paul were making is that the sacrifices, which please God, are only those he has requested of us. That is, when we set out by ourselves to determine what has sacrificial value we are being prideful, self-righteous, and rebellious. We are placing a price on obedience. We are allowing our heart to be led by our mind, we are choosing to love self over God, and that is the trap Saul fell into.

Obedience is the reverential face of faith. It is the result of placing God's desire for our lives ahead of the material cravings our worldly selves cry out for. Obedience turns a deaf ear to the world and refuses the pleading, compromising, rationalizing sacrificial manipulations that our worldly selves unceasingly plot. Simply, obedience is love of God. Sacrifice is love of self. Obedience is saying no, sacrifice is begging maybe. Obedience is once and for all. Sacrifice is just long enough to forget. Obedience is devoted. Sacrifice is casual.

Obedience is from the heart. Sacrifice is from the mind. Obedience is Abraham. Sacrifice is the rich man. Obedience is repentance. Sacrifice is excuses. Obedience is Jesus Christ. Sacrifice is anyone or anything less. Make no mistake, substituting anything over obedience, whether or not it is readily handy, or comfortable, or socially acceptable or even painful to a degree is still disobedience, and it is starkly, consciously, rebelliously disobedient. The result, as Saul soon discovered is rejection, rejection of the worst form.

It is so difficult at times to make that call, to delineate what I know to be God's plan in my life and what seems natural or convenient at the moment. I want to follow but my immediate circumstances often make leading seem less risky. The problem is that all those little decisions I make on a daily basis that appear to be successful add up to the impression that I actually know what I'm doing and that's right where Satan wants me, playing by his rules and measuring my success by his criteria. That's when I begin to "sacrifice" what were probably meaningless objects in my life as an insincere and inadequate show of obedience.

That's when I have placed a price on obedience. A little pain now for immediate satisfaction becomes the deal I unilaterally make with God to put off or ignore the obedience I know is better. When these times arise, and they do so every day, I try to remind myself that obedience is intending for God, sacrifice is intending for self. When I am the object of my intentions the ultimate limit for improvement or growth becomes restricted to me,

I cannot exceed self, but when God is the object of my intentions there can be no limit. In order to be obedient I must love my Lord with all my heart, all my soul, and all my strength, and that is more pleasing than any sacrifice.

"If any of you wants to be my follower, you must turn from your selfish ways, take up your cross, and follow me. If you try to hang onto your life, you will lose it. But if you give up your life for my sake, you will save it. And what do you benefit if you gain the whole world but lose your own soul? Is anything worth more than your soul?"
Matthew 16:24-26

"Trust in the Lord with all your heart; do not depend on your own understanding. Seek his will in all you do, and he will show you which path to take. Don't be impressed with your own wisdom. Instead, fear the Lord and turn away from evil".
Proverbs 3:5-7

"I want you to show love, not offer sacrifices. I want you to know me more than I want burnt offerings".
Hosea 6:6

CHAPTER 16

"Confidence From Within"

"My grace is all you need. My power works best in weakness."
                                    2 Cor 12:9

I confess. I dread having to speak before a group of people. My short list of acceptable alternatives is infinite, and in fact anything else would be just fine, including imprisonment if it were not too long and the food was okay. Seriously though, it's universal, don't we all have at least one thing, one phobia that just thinking about leaves us clammy-handed. It's as though every other aspect of our lives is on cruise control and then, bam, out of nowhere comes our good ole' buddy, whatever that happens to be, and we're left paralyzed with fear. Some of us handle it better than others, they don't pass out, but deep down inside a twisted creature lurks in everyone that loves to control us, to intimidate us.

So what's the ideal strategy? How do I move forward with confidence while this weakness, this thorn in my side threatens to disrupt my most determined efforts? How do I turn this lifelong deficit, this birth defect, into an asset, a confidence builder that not only will equip me to handle those scary moments, but strengthen me in all other aspects of my life as well? Not surprisingly, Scripture offers radical advice. In no uncertain terms it tells us to embrace this weakness, to welcome it and to let it change our lives in wondrous ways.

Why would anyone ever want to be weak, to develop a weakness, or let alone even admit weakness, especially in today's world where image and perception mean everything? Confidence, or at least the show of it, both inside and out are so crucial in the harsh world of minuscule differences separating success from failure. The modern "all-in" philosophy requires nerves of steel, nerves, which cannot be trusted without a healthy dose of confidence. How can I succeed in the daily war for advantage and gain if I can't even lead myself? How can being weak, appearing weak, or desiring to be weak have any capacity for producing power in my life? How does one spin weakness into power?

The answer is by first realizing and acting on the knowledge that we begin life incomplete, that we are born with an empty spot in the center of our hearts, which can be repaired in only one way. Then, and only then, can the crucial next step be taken in faith. Sure, it takes a leap of faith, but ironically, faith builds confidence. It is integral to confidence. The word confidence means to share or have faith with. When we confide with another, we are sharing our hearts through faith. By definition confidence is not a unilateral relationship. To have confidence implies trust and faith in something or someone outside ourselves that can compensate for or propitiate our intrinsic weakness. Scripture tells us that the solution to lack of confidence is found in a foundational relationship with Christ. So, specifically, from where does our confidence arise?

It helps to begin with considering where confidence does not come from and that means a sober look at the lifelong strategies that most of us apply on a daily basis without ever realizing their destructive potential. Just for starters, confidence does not come from the flesh, the material, sensual world. The quickest way to by-pass all rational thought is to put the pleasure side of our brains in control, without limitation or conscious oversight, and then expect anything but bad to result. The Bible tells us that, "I am all too human, a slave to sin". We can honestly want to do the right thing, but the sin nature inside us will always prevail. You only have to look at the epidemic levels of obesity, alcohol and drug dependence, pornography, and moral relativism to grasp the overwhelmingly destructive effects of unbridled sensuality. The Good News though is that the answer is in Jesus Christ, if we only take the time to mute our sensory overload just long enough to allow the Holy Spirit a chance to rescue us and guide us. Placing faith in the material world is never a successful strategy or solution, it may dull our pain or delay the inevitable for today, but there are no worldly short cuts to faith, only short circuits.

Confidence cannot arise from our good works either. Repeat that? It's the truth. Good works won't earn heaven, or even an "Atta boy" from the Lord. Good works are necessary and to be commended, but apart from faith they have no lasting quality. What that means is that anyone can obey the Law, can live a "moral" life, can boast of a multitude of good deeds, but on Judgment Day they will be of no avail because the only act that God asks of us is to believe in his Son. However, once we are living in faith our works become our fruit, they are inspired by and directed by the Holy Spirit. It is these works, which will be judged, not those from before our salvation, and it is these works, which Christ will know us by. Isn't that a liberating promise? Talk about building confidence. I no longer have to worry about being good enough, or of having been too bad. I am no longer compelled to self-reliance. I only have to accept the simple, humble gift of life, and follow His path to success.

Another place not to put your confidence is in your associations, your circle of friends and family, those whom you work with or anyone else for that matter who is not of the body of Christ. Neither their faith nor lack thereof can play any role in where you stand in the eyes of God. That's fairly tough to consider I know, but God shows no favoritism, he accepts those who fear him and do what is right, and that's it. There is no middle ground. There is no place where people can wait while deciding, or wait in hopes of a "better deal". For those who rely on the goodness of others they may have known, or who accept unsound spiritual leadership, or just wait until it is too late, there is no glory only endless regret. If I were prone to a lack of confidence, it would be this revelation alone that would demand action on my part. Fight or flight is not a successful survival reflex in spiritual matters; on this point of confidence the answer is found within ourselves only when once we have invited the answer to enter.

Those are most of the places where not to look. So what about the where? Where does a weakness dwell which could grow confidence? From what inherent characteristic or trait could it possibly spring? If its not from within my self-reliant self, then where? The Bible teaches us that it is found in the sin nature and lack of faith that we are born with. These two birth defects establish the critical, fundamental weakness shared by all mankind prior to God's gift of grace.

Thankfully though, Scripture teaches four broad and interconnected foundations, which serve to establish as well as preserve our trust and faith in Christ. The first and most important of these is salvation. "My grace is all you need, do not be afraid, for I have ransomed you. I have called you by name; you are mine". Salvation does not come from within, but reconciles the weakness from within. My salvation pardons my sin, it resolves my shame, it negates my self-righteousness, it ends my separation from God and it denies the constant accusations that come from Satan. Salvation does not just go a long way towards these goals. It goes all the way. It puts Christ in me and with Christ as my guide how can I lack even the smallest degree of confidence? Christ said, "If you had faith even as small as a mustard seed, you could say to this mountain, 'move from here to there', and it would move. Nothing would be impossible". How's that for a promise from the maker of the universe and everything in it? Salvation assures our confidence by overcoming the weakness of self-reliance.

Once saved, God gives us his gift of the Holy Spirit as an indwelling presence reassuring us of his promise that we are his children. His Spirit joins with our spirit to affirm that we are his, and he is with us wherever we go, that he goes before us and comes alongside us through all the days of our lives. And if we get the big head from time to time, his Spirit is there to teach us what is true and to make us realize what is wrong in our lives. It corrects us when we are wrong and teaches us to do what is right. The Holy Spirit is ever our intercessor and our guide. It is that positive voice that encourages our good works, clarifies our prayers, convicts our transgressions, assures us of salvation, empowers us to serve God's purpose in our lives, and helps us to carry the Word to all the nations. The Holy Spirit directs our confidence by redeeming the weakness of being lost.

The trials and troubles of life play a crucial role in developing confidence. James advises, *"When troubles come your way, consider it an opportunity for great joy. For you know that when your faith is tested, your endurance has a chance to grow."* Our trials serve to build confidence through endurance and perseverance. As we grow through trials, others are heartened and drawn to Christ. There is a certain comfort in knowing that others are taking note on how we respond to the difficulties in life and that our positive response ultimately wins souls to Christ, it builds our confidence. Trials are selected specifically for us and intended to shape us and bring us closer to God. He knew us while we were still in our mother's womb. Therefore he must know all the days of our lives. Trials reveal our trust in Christ and separate us from our material dependence. Christ promised that our trials would never be more than we could endure. That knowledge serves to build confidence for when the tough times arrive, and they inevitably do. Trials strengthen our confidence by exposing the weakness of pride.

Lastly, our confidence is realized through prayer. Paul taught us, "Don't worry about anything, instead, pray about everything. Tell God what you need, and thank him for all he has done." Prayer defines my relationship with God; it places him on the throne and me at the foot. Prayer brings me peace by placing all my concerns under God's care. It delivers me from insecurity, uncertainty and indecision. Being in constant, daily prayer demonstrates my great hope. Christ asked, "How can I receive what I have not asked for?" That says it all. When we seek God's design in our lives and he responds with direction how can we help but be confident in the outcome? Prayer strengthens our confidence by confessing the weakness of sin.

Confidence comes from confiding with Christ, from sharing and trusting our hearts to Christ. It can be a daunting challenge on the one hand to give up control, to finally realize that I don't have all the answers, that I can't really see what lies ahead, that the universe doesn't revolve around me. But when that moment arrives, when we finally and joyfully let go of ourselves and ask

Christ to enter in, he runs to us and takes us by the hand, having known all along that all we ever really wanted was to be loved, to know and to be known, and to confide in the One who loved us enough to make it all possible.

"You will keep in perfect peace those whose minds are steadfast because they trust in you."
                                    Isaiah 26:3

CHAPTER 17

"But I Miss My Old Life"

"This means that anyone who belongs to Christ has become a new person. The old life is gone; a new life has begun".
                    2 Cor 5:17

Being alive is all about change, but as creatures of habit every new "whatever" is met with a certain amount of skepticism, of worry, and of longing for the past. It's only natural to want to stick with what works, with the familiar things in life. The law of survival insists on an experiential discovery of successful strategy followed by a dedicated adherence to its almost certain outcome, at least until that outcome fails to materialize. Then what? Psychologists tell us that those who are willing to fail (i.e. take a risk) are most likely to succeed. Einstein defined an idiot as one who insisted, beyond all evidence to the contrary, on attempting the same failed strategy over and over again while expecting a different result.

Another way of looking at it, or not, is like the person who "buries their head in the sand", refusing to acknowledge reality by taking unreal measures to escape it. This primitive survival characteristic, this fear of change, this stubbornness, has over time, evolved into elaborate societal strategies. But these paradigms and memes are uniquely human constructs, which serve more to indoctrinate and conform the mind and soul than to empower them. It takes a spiritual revolution to be unbound. Jesus said, "If any of you wants to be my follower, you must turn from your selfish ways, take up your cross daily, and follow me. If you try to hang onto your life, you will lose it. But if you give up your life for my sake, you will save it".

Change, or the very thought of change is discouraged from the top down, in every aspect of our lives. Inevitably, most "normal" people are unwilling to make a major alteration in their lives until they feel they have no choice, and even then the decision they often make is to accept the first available option. This is generally not such a successful strategy. So, why are we so reluctant as human beings to embrace change, to let go our fearful grip on the status quo and to celebrate the infinite promise of the future with willing hearts?

The answer emerges from two aspects of our lives, which, if not coordinated, will always produce a conflict, both practically as well as spiritually. The deafening clamor of our physical, material world, if left unchecked, will almost always drown out the patient, humble whisper of our souls. Scripture says it this way, "Don't be drunk with wine, because that will ruin your life. Instead, be filled with the Holy Spirit". Don't let the immediacy of our worldly lives prevent us from the fulfillment of our spiritual lives. Don't accentuate the material, sensual, prideful world over the Truth. This is easier said than done, especially when we find ourselves embroiled in the day-to-day struggles that exemplify modern (whatever that is) life. But is it really honest to say, much less believe, that one's worldly concerns supersede his or her spiritual concerns? Wouldn't it be so much more acceptable, so much more rewarding if our daily concerns were less our own personal responsibility and more those of the Creator of the universe? Who should you trust more, yourself or the One who knew you before you were born, who set you apart and appointed you? Sound impossible? Christ said that what is impossible for people, is always possible with God.

So what comes next now that we have quieted our hearts and shut off the status quo monitor alarm, now that change is the possible, if not the desirable outcome? Paul wrote, "Don't copy the behavior and customs of this world, but let God transform you into a new person by changing the way you think. Then you will learn to know God's will for you, which is good and pleasing and perfect". Good and pleasing and perfect are the characteristics of an ideal life, on that point most of us would agree. Imagine, I never have to be concerned if this or that decision is the correct one because I have committed all of the responsibility to the only authority in the universe that knows beforehand all of the variables that influence it's outcome. It's sort of like cheating, like having the answer before you even ask the question.

How awesome is that? So how do I know what God has planned for me, what pleases God most in my life, what can I do to escape from this relentless pressure that the world is applying? Scripture tells us, "Don't worry about anything, instead, pray about everything. Tell God what you need, and thank him for all he has done. Then you will experience God's peace, which exceeds anything we can understand". Yes, it is that simple. Repent, pray and praise. Allow the Word in, allow the Spirit to speak, allow your life to unfold in the way it was intended and suddenly you find yourself no longer addressing the same old dead-end, able to see with the blinders removed and, most importantly, no longer looking to the past as a goal, but rather as an achievement, a step successfully taken.

It is only natural and healthy to reflect on the decisions we make in life. It is a part of learning how to cope in the physical world. Every act we take establishes the present, defines the past, and restricts the future. Time demands that all of our decisions are irrevocable, they are based on insufficient data, and they are never final. The most powerful computer man could ever devise, using the most advanced software he could ever write, addressing the most simple question the world could ever ask will never produce or even approximate the perfection that God promises through his word. Yes, there is a certain amount of security that can be found in memories and those things and activities that define us as an individual, but ultimately they are worldly and only separate us from true security. It is only through God's amazing grace that security can be obtained worry-free.

The important thing is to listen to the Holy Spirit within you, who will guide you toward those things that encourage the deepening of your relationship with God, and away from those things that hinder that relationship. Let the Spirit be your guide, and your step will always be true. That is a truth you can always trust. Seek Christian fellowship, find an "Alive" church, encourage the Holy Spirit to "light your path", accept God's discipline into your life and don't be prideful. Do these things and you will achieve the impossible. Do these things and you will never miss your old life, you will cherish your "new".

"Because the Sovereign Lord helps me, I will not be disgraced. Therefore, I have set my face like a stone, determined to do his will. And I know that I will not be put to shame".
Isaiah 50:7

CHAPTER 18

"Self Reliance"

"No, Peter protested, you will never ever wash my feet! Jesus replied, 'Unless I wash you, you won't belong to me".

John 13:8

The noted American philosopher and writer Ralph Waldo Emerson is perhaps best known for his essay "Self Reliance". It was completed in 1841 and published along with a collection of controversial articles presenting his views on man's spiritual individuality and unique "virtue". While rejecting his lifelong Unitarian foundation, which denied the Holy Trinity and salvation through Christ, this essay marked Emerson as a pioneer in the American Transcendental Movement. Transcendentalists argued the inherent goodness of man and the ultimate corruptive nature that organized political and religious institutions in society eventuate.

Emerson grandly declared, "no law can be sacred to me but that of my nature ... God is here within". As a graduate and representative of The Harvard Divinity School these views were met with open, disputative hostility from both the educational leadership as well as the popular "intelligentsia" of the time. Although Emerson's radical departure from the tenets of Unitarianism was bold, the true revolutionary concept that he unintentionally initiated was the existence of a personal, in-dwelling God, and this idea was a game changer. To "Dare to love God, without mediator or veil", was his radical challenge to a lukewarm and rote church authority. At the time, this concept was courageous enough, but had he rightly identified this unique "virtue" as the Holy Spirit, an in-dwelling gift from God, that would have been monumental.

In one regard Emerson should be congratulated for turning away from a stagnant religion long enough to address this individual spiritual character of virtue or "intuition", but he faltered, and rather than credit those gifts to a benevolent Father he attributed them to man himself. He became self-reliant. On the one hand he escaped the worldly perils of rite and tradition, but in congratulating himself he never beheld "the last fact behind which analysis cannot go". He sensed the presence of the in-dwelling Holy Spirit, but he failed to appreciate it, and in doing so he allowed his greatest essay to fall short.

All too often we commit ourselves to a tremendous undertaking and then, within reach of triumph, we sell ourselves short by smiling into the mirror rather than pushing past. It is so very difficult to achieve, to be successful, to witness the positive attributes of one's actions and not fall victim to pride, to take all the credit where none is due. It is the human thing to do. It's the "natural" opposite of our response to hardships. Extreme circumstances beget extreme reactions and conditions that place us in imminent peril or elicit strong emotional reactions are especially pernicious in that regard. They tend to force us inward, seeking for clues from past experience, hoping to discover some long-forgotten miraculous talent or strength of character from which we can extricate ourselves out of the immediate threat. It's the psychological version of curling up in a ball. It's a defense through denial.

Regrettably, men seem to oscillate between these extremes, self-reliance and defiance. But ultimately they are two sides of the same coin. It's all-in no matter what, that's the result we should expect when we are reactive rather than proactive. Reactive is reflexive, is physical and worldly. Proactive is reflective, is faithful and holy. The self-reliant Emerson made a case for the independent man, armed in biblical virtue, freed from the shackles of societal institutions when he pronounced, "Whoso would be a man must be a non-conformist", "Self-existence is the attribute of the Supreme Cause". He was on the right track, he just ran out of road.

Man has often sold himself short since the Garden of Eden, since he wed himself to the world. Christ came to earth to release man from his near-sighted spiritual shackles, but he also came to instruct us not to allow the overwhelming volume of our worldly experience to deafen us to the graceful, lifesaving encouragements of our heavenly Father. No other disciple carried this burden more honestly or clumsily than Peter, and perhaps that is why Christ chose him for one final appeal to man's hubris. The apostle John recorded a scene from the Last Supper, which exemplifies the perils of Peter's self-reliance in unforgettable terms. It was a scene overlooked, or at least not mentioned by the other apostles, possibly because it was so unexpected, so unlike all of the other occasions where Christ was appealing to his disciples on terms and in ways that even today we are just beginning to appreciate. It was a scene of complete humility, of love, of forgiveness, of encouragement, but most importantly it was a scene of denial. It was the moment when Jesus washed the feet of his disciples. John recalled the details as follows:

So he got up from the table, took off his robe, wrapped a towel around his waist, and poured water into a basin. Then he began to wash the Disciple's feet, drying them with the towel he had around him. When Jesus came to Simon Peter, Peter said to him, "Lord, are you going to wash my feet?" Jesus replied, "You don't understand now what I am doing, but someday you will". "No", Peter protested, "You will never ever wash my feet!" Jesus replied, "Unless I wash you, you won't belong to me."
John 13:4-8

Like so many of us, Peter was hobbled with a self-centered attitude throughout his life, never really appreciating the essential ingredient he required for his faith to be complete. He was willing to follow Christ, to separate himself from an unbelieving society, even to fight Roman soldiers, but each time his resolve was tested, his absolute, unquestioning dependence on Christ, Peter fell back into self-reliance. He was a man of action until real action was needed. This is subtle denial, not the up-front-in-your-face version like "I don't know him". In many ways this is worse, this is like, "I know you, but I don't believe you."

This is fair weather faith, untested and unclaimed, lukewarm and rote. In a sense, Peter was in the same place as Emerson, he knew God and he cherished God's presence in his life, but he stopped short of fully committing, of being all-in by always insisting on making the final move. Christ offers to wash our feet each and every day of our lives, to accept his humble grace, to drop our defensive postures and to be cleansed in the only blood, which has redemptive value. If we are sincere in our professed hope in a redeemer, in the coming Messiah, then how do we reconcile this hope with the rejection that characterizes most of us through our daily lives?

Our denial may not be the overt, demonstrative, wear-it-on-my-chest kind of rejection, but a more subtle form, couched in independence and pride, far less showy and infinitely more destructive. Look at it as a barrier, a man-made worldly and spiritual construct that separates us from our Creator.

The Last Supper was one final opportunity for Christ to impart to his disciples an essential belief, this requirement of total obedience. His message was clear, denial waits patiently in every moment of our lives. This brief confrontation between Christ and his favorite headstrong disciple, forgotten or not noted by all of the others that night except John, when compared against the later prediction of three frank denials in one night, illustrates the subtle face of self-reliance that we must always be sensitive to. Whenever I catch myself saying, "I've got this", it's helpful to remember Peter and to be encouraged through his example of God's infinite patience, even in the most humble of settings.

"Don't worry about anything; instead, pray about everything. Tell God what you need, and thank him for all he has done".
Philippians 4:6

CHAPTER 19

"Why Must I Suffer?"

"I know that you can do anything and that no one can stop you. You asked, "Who is this that questions my wisdom with such ignorance?" It is I, and I was talking about things I knew nothing about, things far too wonderful for me."
                                         Job 42:2-3

Imagine a world in which there was only one color, one sound, one smell, one flavor, one taste, or one of any or everything. Now, imagine trying to describe where you are or what you are hearing, or what you see or smell. How do you describe the color red in a world where everything is entirely blue, and how do you know everything is blue when there is no other "color" to compare from? In fact, can color even exist in that world? Another way of looking at it would be to attempt mathematics with only one number. How do we construct any other number when only one is available or possible? What would one plus one equal? Could mathematics even exist on a single point? How can any sense be useful or possible in a one-dimensional world? How can any comparison be made? In fact, can we even attempt or understand the concept of comparison in a one-dimensional world.

In order for our natural world to have any variety at all, or for sentient beings to be able to describe this world in any meaningful, reality-based way there must "per force" be more than one dimension, one shade, one flavor, one number etcetera from which to begin. It is this inviolate condition, that the physical world, in order for it to exist, must be comprised of a range, an infinite range of possibilities and probabilities that condemns us to a world of extremes. The range of colors is infinite as are the ranges of sound, smell, taste and any other natural physical descriptive property, and so, by default, are the "states" of existence that we find ourselves bound to. The added dimension of time insures that these "states" are in a constant and infinite process of change and we, as sentient human beings, are fundamentally defined by this reality. Yesterday became today, which in turn will become tomorrow. Light becomes dark, dark becomes light. Hot becomes cold, cold becomes hot. For every action there is an opposite and equal reaction and the "randomness" of our universe is constantly increasing. In fact, there is likely more than one "uni"-verse. So it should come as no surprise that the range of physical states and conditions and extremes that man can find self in is infinite as well.

A one-dimensional world in which everything was blue, or tasted like vanilla, or felt cool or was light could not exist in terms we can define because they would have no objectivity, no absolute basis from which to refer from. A world of one-dimensional character would just "be", it could be anything you chose, but without choices it would just "be". In a one-dimensional universe everything would be the same for everyone, and everyone would be the same. Life in a one-dimensional world would exist as a single moment of time and would have neither a past nor a future, in fact the present would not be the present, it would just be. In order for you or I to make or create any choice in this world we would have to accept along with that choice, its options, which would be infinite - some of those options would be "better" than the choice we made while others would be "worse". Also, and of critical importance, would be the interjection of time; for in order for one state of being to change into another time must elapse. Enter mortality, and enter good and bad. Enter colors, smells, tastes, and sensations. Enter hot, cold, hungry, and full. Enter up, down, high and low. Enter pain and enter ecstasy. Enter the awesome range, the infinite possibilities of our physical world. With each choice we make exists already an infinite set of options from which to choose, each with its own potential future in its own potential universe. If we consider for a moment the enormity of infinity, the potential for goodness is without limits, but so too can be the potential for evil. Or can it?

On the sixth day of creation God formed man from the dust of the ground and planted the garden in Eden where he placed the man he had made. In the middle of the garden he placed the tree of life and the tree of the knowledge of good and evil. At the end of the sixth day God looked over all that he had made and he saw that it was very good. Although evil already existed, it was the prideful acts of Adam and Eve who ate of the forbidden fruit of the tree of the knowledge of good and evil that first introduced sin into man's world. The potential for sin was just as infinite as was the potential for good, however this unrighteous state of sin separated man from God.

But God loved the world so much that he gave his one and only Son as propitiation for sin, so that everyone who believes in him will not perish but have eternal life. Sin became finite through Christ. Christ overcame all the sin, which had ever existed or will ever exist and defeated it on the Cross. Christ arose on the third day and entered into heaven sinless where he awaits our presence and prepares for his glorious return. The infinite quantity of good now reigns over the finite quantity of evil, and although evil and suffering still characterize our human existence we can be assured in our hope that through God's grace they will end, and goodness will reign forever. So, we can rejoice when we run into problems and trials, for we know that they help us develop endurance. And endurance develops strength of character, and character strengthens our confident hope of salvation. And this hope will not lead to disappointment. For we know how dearly God loves us because he has given us the Holy Spirit to fill our hearts with his love. Perhaps Job expressed man's best and most positive response to suffering.

"I came naked from my mother's womb, and I will be naked when I leave. The Lord gave me what I have, and the Lord has taken it away. Praise the name of the Lord!"   Job 1:21

God allowed Satan to test Job's faith, to deprive him of all of his worldly possessions, his family and friends and eventually from his health. Satan had argued that Job's faith arose from God's blessings and prosperity, that Job's fear of God was a matter of convenience, not faith, that Job was a fair weather believer. Job survived all that Satan could throw at him and although he was stressed to the limit, to the point of giving up and begging for death, his final act was capitulation and repentance. His final act was a profession of faith and God blessed him for it.

It's helpful, in fact it's imperative, that when we find ourselves in times of stress to be confident in three indisputable facts. Firstly, God loves us. We are his chosen people and ultimately his bride. He is faithful and patient in correcting us as preparation in our new selves. Secondly, God does not sin, he may allow sin and suffering into our lives, but he is not it's cause. Adam and Eve ate the fruit at Satan's bequest and as a result we are borne into a sin state. It is God's grace and Christ's sacrifice, which offer our only redemption. And thirdly, it is entirely human to avoid sin and suffering - to abhor its presence in our lives. Even Christ asked to be spared this suffering, but chose through faith to place God's will above his own. It was this unselfish, humble, faithful sacrifice that gives each of us the hope and confidence that sin and suffering are finite, they have been overcome, that they will end in our lives.

"He went a little farther and bowed with his face to the ground, praying, 'My Father. If it is possible, let this cup of suffering be taken away from me. Yet I want your will to be done, not mine."

Matthew 26:39

CHAPTER 20

"A Monument Not Shaped By Human Hands"

"We will not hide these truths from our children; we will tell the next generation about the glorious deeds of the Lord, about his power and his mighty wonders."
                                                    Psalm 78:4

This past year has been a constant unrelenting grind. Sickness, surgeries, multiple challenges at work, and with each of our three children facing serious struggles themselves there was real crisis and unrest no matter where we turned. For years it seemed Kathy and I were always ready to handle unwelcome turns with assurance. Problems would present themselves and we would shrug them off with hardly a thought. Problems felt physical and temporary. They were never appreciated as the spiritual challenges they actually turned out to be, and no matter how bad our trials seemed, I honestly don't think I ever saw them as assaults on faith. The Bible teaches differently though, trials exist only to mold and refine us. Trials are our crucible, the defining moments of life. Their impact on faith cannot be postponed forever. If I've learned anything in my walk, experience warns that, "what goes up, must come down". This our sixty-second year has slogged progressively down. But I get it, everyone eventually experiences deep troubles in life. So ironically, this devotional is not about complaint, in fact, it is just the opposite. It is my joyous declaration of the power of triumphant faith, of transformative faith, and of monumental faith.

For most of my lifetime, hardships, while huge in their own way, never quite caught my full attention. They burned brightly for a time and then were lost to the noise of self-reliance and pride. But God is patient and he knew this year was coming. He also knew the only sure way through was "a pathway no one knew was there", the path of faith. This year especially, he has been patient to lead me away from myself, from the worry of the moment, and to recall the wonderful deeds He has graced me with throughout my life. As a couple, realizing the significance of those blessings has been the single most redemptive thought we have focused on and prayed about all this year. The confident hope that God has gone before us and that he has personally prepared the way, a path that others would come to see and in turn be inspired by, has been our rock.

When our circumstances seemed the most difficult, when it seemed that every traumatic moment lingered as if to heighten its fearful pain, we found the only reliable source of peace was in counting God's awesome blessings, in keeping them constantly in our prayers, always faithfully trusting that how we responded would serve as an example to others.

The nation of Israel was released from four centuries of slavery in Egypt and had wandered the deserts east of Canaan for another forty years when Joshua was called by God to lead them across the Jordan River. Many times during that wilderness period the Israelites had approached this point only to fail because of their fears and shallow faith. Patiently, God had allowed them to wander, aimless in their disobedience, even though many perished despite his provision. In fact, none of the original Israelites who had survived Egypt were left alive when the chosen day to cross the Jordan finally arrived, except for Joshua and Caleb.

Throughout those forty years these two men had remained faithful and obedient, and it was Joshua that God called on to make the final push. Among his non-negotiable instructions, Joshua was ordered to build two memorials as reminders of the Lord's miraculous intervention that day. Specifically, they were to be gathered from the middle of the riverbed and built of stones unaltered by human hands. God declared the purpose of the memorials was to remind the Israeli children of the day the Jordan River stopped flowing, and of the miracle when the Ark of the Lord's Covenant led their people to the Promised Land. God also promised the stones would stand forever.

From earliest recorded time, human civilizations have raised up monuments. Prideful edifices dedicated to posterity and yet destined to mediocrity. The greatest material works that man has achieved eventually fall though, weathered and shattered, strewn throughout the world like so many forgotten toys. In Solomon's words, the sum total of man's permanent impact on this material world has been meaningless, like chasing the wind, but not those of the Lord. A skeptic might challenge, "Where are these holy monuments? Where are the memorials that mark God's miracles for all to see? Where are the stones that God promised would stand forever? And the simple answer lies right before us each and every day. It is the miracles in our lives and more specifically, it is the changed lives that others experience through them. God's monuments are the decisions, the acts of obedience, the faith without seeing, and the mighty works which they produce that are witnessed by our children, our co-workers, and the people we encounter everyday. God's monuments are his promises and his blessings brought mercifully to life, one redeemed soul at a time.

Our year began in hardship. It took a miracle and the humble acknowledgement of his wonderful deeds in our lives to put us right. Psalm seventy-seven describes the ordeal perfectly. It is a song of incredible joy, yet it first arises from the agony of despair. The disconsolate verses which mark it's beginning convicted me of my self-centeredness and aversion to hardship. But its triumphant close confirmed God's wonderful deeds and our responsibility to tell our family and friends. The verses in between are a primer on any man's natural reaction to trials and just how dark it can become when we choose self-reliance over obedience. From rejection to sleeplessness, from abandonment to remorse, the full range of our quiet desperation was unmasked. The turning point arrived when we gave up on self and rightfully credited all the wonders he has blessed us with. It was in that moment that our past was finally, mercifully forgiven and his miraculous path could be revealed. We went from dreading each day to looking forward to what each new day would have in store. We went from half empty to half full and haven't looked back.

God brings his people to an "impossible" place to demonstrate his power and to strengthen their faith, so that others might see his work through them. It is in those moments that the miracles in our lives become the monuments in the lives of our family and friends, and that is only possible through grace. Although our trials have been many and diverse this year, comparing trials is like comparing scars, it's superficial and it's impossible. A scar, no matter the story, is just the evidence of survival, nothing more. It neither tells the tale, nor augurs the future, unless it is a scar suffered in faith and obedience, in which case its effect becomes a constructive part of the crucible which shapes us and the faith of those whom we live to influence. It is then, just as He promised, that hardship becomes more than just a scar, it becomes a permanent memorial and a living, willing testimony to others.

"We were crushed and overwhelmed beyond our ability to endure, and we thought we would never live through it. In fact, we expected to die. But as a result, we stopped relying on ourselves and learned to rely on God, who raises the dead."
                                            2 Corinthians 1:8-9

CHAPTER 21

"What Will Suffice?"

"He has given me a new song to sing, a hymn of praise to our God. Many will see what he has done and be amazed. They will put their trust in the Lord."   Psalm 40:3

It seems more and more today that we have abandoned the art of giving, of suffering some small sacrifice to self in order to enhance the life of another. Sometimes we even have difficulty in saying thank you when those rare moments happen in our favor, when someone else has actually suffered freely for us. Regrettably, our contemporary version of respect seems based not so much on honest personal relationships as it is on arbitrary interactions. Whether through practiced neglect or just plain indifference, respect has become a material test of power rather than a spiritual sense of obligation. Giving back is therefore, anathema. Bottom line, the simple act of being grateful is no longer considered an asset but rather a weakness in many circles. If a gift is not taken for granted, it's often taken by force, and either way the decision seems based strictly on, "what's it worth, what's in it for me?"

In so many selfish ways we have grown complacent to the daily miracles that define our lives, only to neglect the simple, humble acts of recognition, of acknowledging the unconditional source of their beneficence. The loss, or worse, the denial of that sense of indebtedness, fosters a self-righteous attitude, and what should have been a positive influence in our lives becomes sadly corrupted. So how do I respond when charity falls my way? Besides the momentary thankful pause, the wistful smile, the sigh of relief, what authentic, public acknowledgement should I offer that would reflect even the slightest hint of my obligation? How do I humbly give thanks for that which I do not naturally deserve? Specifically, does it change me or do I remain the same?

    It was into this world of spontaneous, constantly shifting moral relativity, where the bizarre happily masquerades as the normal, that Jesus arrived one morning after crossing a stormy lake from Galilee. Scripture tells us that he was just stepping out of his battered boat when a man, who was possessed by demons, approached him. Luke says the man was "homeless and naked, and living in a cemetery outside of town." As soon as he saw Jesus, he shrieked and fell down in front of him. Then he demanded, "Why are you interfering with me, Jesus, Son of the Most High God? Please, I beg you, don't torture me!"
    The man was named Legion in lieu of the many demons he harbored. The surreal, almost unbelievable story that day of the confrontation of Jesus with those demons and their frantic supplication and miraculous purge, generated news which should have comforted and evoked joy on the part of the villagers who were witness to it. But instead, this miracle was met with open hostility. The Bible tells us that the townspeople

actually begged Jesus to go away and leave them alone, "for a great wave of fear had swept over them." Strangely though, the once possessed man, who was seen sitting at Jesus' feet, fully clothed and perfectly sane, pleaded instead to go with him.

So, how does a miracle generate such opposite reactions? How do fear and affection arise from the same source? Why would some want more of the miracle while others be so adamant to be left without? In other words, how can some of us respond to a gift with gratitude, while others just ignore it or reject it outright?

The answer lies in how we see the gift. Do we see it as a blessing or as a threat? Does it fulfill us or leave us shamed? Like the demons, who accused Christ of interference and begged not to be "tortured" the townspeople had seen enough of the power of Jesus and had no desire to have their comfortable, self-righteous lives upset. Their response to the free gift of salvation was one of suspicion and selfish denial. They were hard-hearted and skeptical. Repentance and change were not in their cards, but the once-possessed man, "went all through the town proclaiming the great things Jesus had done for him." He was done with worldly chains and spiritual nakedness, he had no difficulty in seeing the value of his gift, and he was unashamed.

One gift, two entirely different responses. One a matter of obligation, the other an act of rejection. One the free gift of grace, the other the priceless cost of refusal. Does this response really reflect the value of the gift or is it more a matter of the heart?

The irony is that the intrinsic value of a gift, free without conditions, often without warning or consideration, can leave it dangerously vulnerable to misinterpretation. That is to say, a gift without established value, by whatever measure, can be taken for granted. After all, if something has been given unconditionally, then it must have no value to the one who has given it, right? And if it has no value then why should I waste my time and effort either accepting it or acknowledging it? But the problem with placing the value of self over all else can prevent us from identifying and accepting a gift greater than self, because in order to receive it we must first diminish self. It's as though self-preservation overrules change so dogmatically that we would be willing to embrace permanent loss over unconditional grace.

Were the townspeople fearful of being sent plunging into the lake like a herd of pigs? Maybe. Or were they really afraid because they would no longer be able to run about naked and in chains like the madman? Probably. Which choice did they fear most? Neither really, although the second would likely be closer to the truth. The fear the townspeople secretly dreaded most was that of change. They selfishly saw fundamental change as a threat. Someone once prophetically wrote, "We change our behavior when the pain of staying the same becomes greater than the pain of changing." The townspeople had no heart for change, they were still comfortable in their chains, and their shame was tethered by their pride.

In a very real sense that's the crux of the problem. When I focus entirely and exclusively on myself, then what I identify as self becomes inseparably valuable and the very thought of parting with anything seen as self can lead to real, visceral discomfort. Self becomes more important than all else, and consciously or not I project that conviction into every decision I make. This self-centered strategy is generally successful until, like the townspeople above, I encounter a gift of inestimable value, especially one that shines undeniable truth onto the falsehoods I have coveted up to that moment. It is in that crucial moment, like the demon-possessed man, that I must make the first move. I must have a heart for change, and I must trust my sins to the One who can send them plunging into the lake. And then, like a man possessed, I must share the Good News. That is the only thank-you that can ever suffice.

"For I have a great sense of obligation to people in both the civilized world and the rest of the world, to the educated and the uneducated alike. So I am eager to come to you in Rome too, to preach the Good News. For I am not ashamed of this Good News about Christ."
Romans 1:14-16

CHAPTER 22

"In Thanksgiving"

"Abba, Father, he cried out, everything is possible for you. Please take this cup of suffering away from me. Yet I want your will to be done, not mine."
Mark 14:36

Traditional history has it that the Pilgrims of Plymouth Colony were the first to celebrate Thanksgiving in the Fall of 1621 after having survived a particularly difficult year marked by draught, starvation and disease, which had left the original settlers with less than half those who had first come to the New World. Admittedly, it was at its core a religious celebration, but the sad truth is, that in the fight for survival to that day, the first Americans resorted to theft and other desperate measures in imposing their will on the native Indian peoples who lived in the area. The local tribes had shared their knowledge of hunting, fishing and cultivation, and were sorely rewarded by the Pilgrims with betrayal.

Our forefathers abandoned their morality when their circumstances became unbearably difficult, and some would say with natural justification, took what they needed by force, ignoring the laws and the truth of the word they had traveled so far and labored so hard to share. They were thankful, but only to a point. They were thankful for the good in their lives, but responded poorly to the bad. They were thankful for God's provision, but not for his tribulation. The Pilgrims did nothing to deserve help from the native Indians, nothing to be boastful of, in fact their actions were just the opposite, and amazingly, rather than the punishment they deserved they were saved through mercy. The world around them was hostile and God made it friendly. God reprieved their sin and their response was to be thankful only for deliverance.

What it should have been was to be thankful for the trials, which had delivered them to the Father in the first place. Isn't it so easy to see only the glorious result when what we should really pay attention to is the holy process?

When we gather together next week with family, when we have safely assembled from all the many distant locations and walks in life we find ourselves bound to, perhaps it is with a certain degree of shame and conviction that we should also remember those who first led us to this day. Perhaps in giving thanks to all the many blessings and good works that we have realized in our lives and the lives of our loved ones, this year we should focus more on the hardships that have come our way and how we have received and responded to them. Although we should recognize and be truly thankful for the merciful goodness in our lives and the daily miracles that greet each of us with every new and hopeful day, it would be a great mistake not to accept them without first joyfully embracing the hard and difficult realities from which they are born.

Like the incessant thorn in Paul's side our trials are intended to bring us closer to God not drive us away. It can be so easy to view the awesome blessings in our lives through the prideful lens of privilege and never really appreciate them for their actual grace, for the ultimate sacrifice and source from which they originally came. It is so easy to fall into nonchalance through the mirage of self-reliance and pride. When once we become transfixed by the stability of our lives, the predictable, comfortable, reassuring routines that most of us strive for, it is always at the cost of losing sight of the provider from which that security arose. Then, when inevitable troubles arrive, our reactions often disavow our professed faith and what we often do under duress does not reflect what we say in leisure. Could that happen because what we have said may never have been faithfully believed? Shouldn't Thanksgiving reflect an appreciation for the grace in our lives rather than the good?

    Life is like this. One night we fall asleep as masters of the universe and then something unpleasant wakes us up. We are in control and then we're not. The world around us seems so chaotic. Threats come from every direction. At times it appears that things couldn't get much worse and you just aren't sure how to respond. When you consider the context of those final hours before Christ was captured and led away to the horrible death which awaited him, when you struggle like he did wanting to be spared at any cost, then just for a moment, the mistakes and poor decisions of our forefathers can seem almost forgivable.

Jesus was in that place the night before his final arrest, he was cornered and had no real options left but to obey. Like any one of us, he did not want to suffer. Sure, he was the Christ, he could have done anything else, and anything he wanted to because he was the Son of Man, the creator of the universe. Instead, he humbly chose to obey. Jesus could have reacted like the Pilgrims did in their days of hardship and conveniently forgotten his life's work and his duty, but thankfully he died for us to grace us with the faith and the prefect example of how to respond to any and all trials we will ever experience. It was his ultimate example of faith and obedience that we should be most thankful for, not the comforts and the security of our lives.

Perhaps the reason why our world seems so daunting today is not so much that it really is, but that we are so apart from its spiritual center. The difference, the perspective that results from being so far away makes the material world seem bigger than it really is. Because we are intractably bound to our immediate worldly concerns their effect can be much greater than it should be. We can't see the forest for the trees. But by drawing closer to God, the world around us begins to lose its ominous significance and our actions will begin to reflect our faith and not our immediate concerns. We can then be led to peace and hope, not to accusation and doubt.

We should be thankful, not so much for our present comforts or the sum of all the awesome gifts we have received through life, because even if there was infinite time to do so we could barely justify those. What Mark tells us, is that what we should honestly and with glad hearts be thankful for, is the gift Christ chose to grace us with, for his sacrifice is impossible to repay. Like our forefathers in Plymouth Colony, we were saved through grace, not for anything we did, but solely for what we believe. Therefore, we must live out that belief, that confident hope. The true message of thanksgiving should be to appreciate that God's gift was freely given, not earned. It was given for those who count their blessings, not in worldly terms, but in those of the spirit. In a true spirit of Thanksgiving we should pray for faith, pray with faith, and thank God for the trials, which brought us to it.

"Keep watch and pray, so that you will not give in to temptation. For the spirit is willing, but the body is weak."
Mark 14:38

"Enjoy prosperity while you can, but when hard times strike, realize that both come from God."
Eccl. 7:14

CHAPTER 23

"Don't Be A One-Hit Wonder"

"But the servant who received the one bag of silver dug a hole in the ground and hid the master's money".
Matthew 25:18

The immortal Margaret Mitchell wrote her masterpiece, "Gone With The Wind", and then mysteriously wrote no more. She died a lonely recluse, the victim of a hit-and-run accident. The avant-garde poet Sylvia Plath published her only book, "The Bell Jar", to immediate and overwhelming acclaim, only to commit suicide one month later. J.D. Salinger, the enigmatic author of "The Catcher In The Rye", rewarded his meteoric rise to literary stardom by becoming a life long recluse, never to publish again. Each of these authors were instant successes, they were read by millions and enjoyed a celebrity and notoriety which most of us could never dream of, yet their follow-up efforts were shallow and at best pitiful. Each writer, in his or her own way accepted the unearned blessing of success and then regrettably quenched it. They responded as though victory begets defeat or affirmation invites condemnation. In each instance opportunity opened an unexpected door only to lead to tragedy.

These three authors shared an all too common trait that transcends every walk of life, from literature to music to sports. It is the problem of initial success followed ironically by rejection and lassitude, or of utter failure. It's very much like being saved from certain death and then selfishly refusing to acknowledge your savior. Those of us unlucky enough never to have experienced the exhilaration of creative genius, might look at these examples and consider them an egregious waste. We might wonder how any rational person, blessed with such awesome talents, could clutch them so tightly, or be so selfish as to never share them again? Or, more to the point, how can God's gifts possibly lead to fear?

Psychologists know it as atychiphobia, the morbid fear of failure. It describes those people who are so bound by their fears that they refuse to take any risk at all. To make matters worse, they are often just as fearful of success and may even subconsciously plot to undermine their own efforts so that they no longer have to make the effort to try. Not only do they doubt their ability to succeed, they actually fear the consequences of success. Incredibly, these poor souls believe that the more exposure one gets through success the more likely it is that they will be uncovered as the frauds they secretly consider themselves to be. Sadly, in an ironic way, the fear of failure might even be considered an exaggerated form of selfishness, of knowing that you have a special gift, but its beauty is so profound that only you yourself could ever fully understand or appreciate it.
Those who suffer from this morbid fear of failure privately have acknowledged their genius, but refuse to live it out, to risk public confirmation.

That's unfortunate, because one's effort eventually determines achievement of personal goals, and therefore this reluctance denies them a lifetime of meaning and the realization of their full potential. So why did they fail? Did they fail because they doubted the cause from which their genius arose, or because they doubted themselves, or because of perceived circumstances beyond their control? Regardless, the net effect is that these tortured souls tend to covet their gifts and avoid sharing them with others. They stop at just one. In both material and spiritual terms, they have taken their treasure and buried it in the ground.

It is exactly this selfish reluctance, this close-minded refusal to share, that Matthew illustrates through Christ's parable of the three servants. It is his aim to reassure each of us that sharing our gifts, investing in them, and enabling them to do the work Christ has planned will necessarily lead to a glorious reward, it will please God greatly. This story clearly teaches us never to accept Christ's precious gift and then harbor it selfishly to ourselves. Matthew warns us, we can and must share it, and we must grow it. But for material beings bound to a material world, that can be a naturally difficult thing to do. So, how best do we share this gift, how do I avoid becoming a "one hit wonder"? How do I resist the fear of failure and rightfully proclaim the fulfillment of faith? What awesome task would I attempt if I knew I could never fail? Better yet, how do I know that I cannot fail?

Not surprisingly, scripture addresses this very issue in Paul's letter to the Romans. Although encouraged by the early Christian's spiritual growth, he was ever alert to their honest fears, and in chapter eight Paul's hard-won observations focus in on three crucial aspects of faith; it's intrinsic potential or strength, the believer's internal perseverance or endurance, and the inherent power or magnitude of the forces at work against us. Specifically, they are: faith in and of itself, one's individual strength in faith, and the final outcome of faith against evil. In developing this broad picture he confronted three universal questions we have all asked at some point weakness of faith. Could we fail because worldly opposition to the Gospel is too great, or could we fail because as individuals we are weak and tend to sin, or could we fail because bad situations overwhelm us in spite of our faith? On closer inspection these three questions closely match the classic characteristics of atychiphobia, that is, insignificance, inadequacy, and inferiority. Those who are crippled by the fear of failure inevitably suffer from one or more of these weaknesses and their lives consequently reflect this battle.

Both the parable of the three servants and Paul's letter offer scriptural advice for confronting our fears. Looking first at whether or not faith is indeed more powerful than the forces aligned against it, his advice is unequivocal, "If God is for us, who can ever be against us". In this one short sentence Paul is declaring God's total sovereignty over the material and spiritual worlds and therefore our invulnerable status as his chosen people. He is encouraging us not to be concerned with the worries of the world for they have already been defeated. For the servant who has buried his treasure in the sand or simply refuses to step outside, the parable reminds us that the material world has no eternal significance, and that we shouldn't behave as though it does. In his letter to the Hebrews he later described it this way, "Because God's children are human beings made of flesh and blood, the Son also became flesh and blood. For only as a human being could he die, and only by dying could he break the power of the devil, who had the power of death". Simply put, the world has no chance, the only way I can possibly fail is to play by its rules, accept its promises, deny the grace of God and just bury my treasure in the sand.

    He then addresses the problem of individual inadequacy or sin with a simple but powerful question, "Who dares accuse us whom God has chosen for his own?" Here Paul is imploring us not to fall into Satan's trap of accusations, that we are forever incapable of waging war alone, that it was never a question of our personal adequacy so much as it was the question of "Who's your daddy?" In his first letter to the Corinthians he explained it this way, "God has united you with Jesus Christ, for our benefit God made him to be wisdom itself. Christ made us right with God, he made us pure and holy, and he freed us from sin". He explains that when we have finally admitted God's amazing grace, we will no longer struggle with being inadequate, because it is no longer the quantity of our acts which matter, but rather the quality of our faith, how we live it out. So for the servant who trusts only himself with God's grace and refuses to share it, the parable of the three servants is warning to us that the only possible way to remain inadequate is to do just that, to conceal God's blessing, to bury it and never allow it to grow in us and for us. Christ is imploring us to invest and prosper through his word, and he promises that our reward will match our trials.

Finally, Paul considers the fear of inferiority. Can our faith fail because our circumstances overwhelm us, or could the world just be too great regardless? In a bold and emphatic voice he declares, "I am convinced that nothing can ever separate us from God's love. Neither death nor life, neither angels or demons, neither our fears for today nor our worries for tomorrow, not even the powers of hell can separate us from God's love". Paul promises God's love for us is greater than the power of this world. Much later John would explain it this way, "But you belong to God, my dear children. You have already won a victory over those people, because the Spirit who lives in you is greater than the spirit who lives in the world". The Spirit, which resides within us, as proof of our salvation is also proof of our superiority over sin and the material world.

Can you ask for any more than that? Or to take it one step further, why would God bless your life with just one gift? So, protected by the full range of faith, by God's sovereignty over the world, by our righteousness in God through Christ, and therefore by our invincibility in the world through the Holy Spirit, how can one ever fear failure? Thankfully, in one of the most reassuring verses of the New Testament Paul encapsulates all we need to know when faced with the enormous task of making sense of these everyday trials of fear. "We know God causes everything to work together for the good of those who love God and are called according to his purpose for them". The bottom line from Matthew and Paul - never let success go to your head and never let failure get to your heart.

"Don't let the wise boast in their wisdom, or the powerful boast in their power, or the rich boast in their riches. But those who wish to boast should boast in this alone: that they truly know me and understand that I am the Lord who demonstrates unfailing love and who brings justice and righteousness to the earth, and that I delight in these things."
Jeremiah 9:23-24

CHAPTER 24

"I'm Stuck"

"Then the disciple Jesus loved said to Peter, 'It's the Lord'. When Simon Peter heard that it was the Lord, he put on his tunic (for he had stripped for work), jumped into the water, and headed for shore."

John 21:7

Doesn't it sound a little odd to be putting on your clothes right before jumping into the water? Why does anyone load themselves up with the extra weight and restrictions that baggy clothes would add before diving headlong into a dangerous sea? In my book, that's a little like asking to be drowned. When I first read this verse several years ago, I'll admit it struck me as unusual, but as sometimes can be the case, I hadn't really welcomed the words with an open heart, so they bounced right off. They registered a bit odd, but I just wasn't patient enough to let the Spirit show me the reason why, and as a result, I walked away from an amazing lesson. It wasn't until this verse worked its way back into a sermon last weekend that the true meaning finally sank in. Mercifully and much to my surprise, this peculiar scene, unusual in an offhand way, would be dovetailed into circumstances that were slowly unfolding in my life. Indeed, as Scripture promises, God's word always produces fruit.

Serendipity, to a large degree, is equal parts patience and preparation, so it helps to be prepared by the One with infinite patience. Have you ever wondered what leads us to recall certain moments from the past as though they were fresh today? Although, at the time there may have appeared no real significance, thankfully some later trigger focuses us on their true meaning. This association, which is so easy to appreciate when things follow closely together, is not so obvious when separated in time. So therefore, when an insight occurs without warning, it tends to be profound. This was the case when this verse spoke to me for the second time.

On the first pass I figured Peter was in a hurry, on the second I understood why. This verse opened my eyes to a problem that dogs me all too often, the problem of becoming spiritually stuck. Like Peter that day, I get stuck in myself and stuck outside of Christ. This verse showed me that it's really a matter of commitment, commitment to the attitude I'm going to wear in life. Do I continue to model the shiny coat of pride or do I humbly reach for the tattered cloak of Christ. And just as Peter demonstrated, this verse told me that in order to become unstuck I must first gird myself in faith. Scripture says the only way to shore is to put on his life jacket.

Painfully, I recall several times growing up, when my mother pointed to a stack of secondhand clothes and ordered me to try them on. As much as I knew I could use them, they were rarely anything I really wanted because they weren't "me", they were always either worn-out or so dated that wearing them was doubly embarrassing. It hurt knowing that she could afford me new clothes, but worse, it hurt that I had to wear stuff that others had rejected. Those were sorry days, having to choose between worn-out or tossed-out, and I still carry the shame of inadequacy and a resentment of not being worthy enough to deserve better. The "old" me was always too good for used. I was all about that spiffy image in the mirror, and never once saw the beauty in a gift not earned. The funny side of the story though is that no matter where I went in my "new" old clothes, people always recognized me as one of Lew's boys. Her loving choices were that unmistakable and that perfect.

So it was only through the grace of forgiving time, and the conviction of this unusual verse, that I finally appreciated my mother's patient design. In order to put on the "new", I had to peel off the "old". In the end, the insults I had imagined and the fears I had cultivated in my childhood turned out to be windmills of pride. Just like Christ's knowledge of Peter, my dear mother knew me better than I knew myself, and short of just telling me so, she still managed to coax me into the right clothes and the right attitude. My mother showed me the only way to wear His tattered life jacket is to take off mine.

The selfish coat of pride has an infinite capacity for accommodation. It fits perfectly anyone willing to bear it, and boasts of comfort in every situation. In fact, it is too comfortable. Pride is so adaptive that you rarely know you have it on, until of course, when God has to peel it off. So wouldn't it be great if you could just feel it when you had it on, or hand it off to someone else, or maybe even throw it away altogether? Unfortunately though, it seems that no matter how hard we try to walk in the light, the dark always finds a way of creeping in. Paul explained it this way in his letter to the Romans, "So I am not the one doing wrong; it is sin living in me that does it."

In that sense, as long as I walk in the world there will be a constant struggle with what attitude to wear, my beautiful coat of pride or the frayed and rejected coat of Christ. That's where Peter was, naked and stuck in his material world yet again, when Christ called him to shore. And like Peter, that's where I often find myself, in a daily struggle with what to wear, to remain myself or to follow without hesitation. Peter showed me the easiest way out of my selfish life jacket is to trust in Christ's.

That's a difficult lesson. Life's experiences have a way of dominating spiritual development, much to our eventual misfortune, especially if we rely solely on the material world for direction and encouragement. Little worries become magnified beyond measure when we are too self-reliant to look outside ourselves for solutions to essential problems. Aren't we often like that though? We may have suffered a trial at some point, which must have seemed significant at the time, and now it's grown a life of its own. It carries this rote, unchallenged, oppressive weight, a feeling that under any other context would be too embarrassing to admit or pointless to defend. And yet, it's just accepted. The material world drowns out the spiritual voice, and then suddenly we're back in our old clothes, our old attitude, and out of the new.

All too often I find myself responding to life's challenges by employing the same tired strategy of trying to solve a problem with my own resources. It's like I'm sleep walking, afraid to face the real world and refusing to wake up to responsibility. And rather than donning the tattered cloak of Christ, I reach into the closet for my "old" pal pride. The result is always the same, an empty boat and a lonely sea. Scripture tells us that the only reliable solution is to react like Peter did and put on the suit that suits the job. For a while that day, Peter was stuck in his material concerns, wearing his day-to-day self-reliance, but when Christ appeared and challenged his motives, he was quick to put on faith and follow. Christ shows me the only way to get unstuck in this life is to put my trust in His.

"Throw off your old sinful nature and your former way of life, which is corrupted by lust and deception. Instead, let the Spirit renew your thoughts and attitudes. Put on your new nature, created to be like God, truly righteous and holy."
Ephesians 4:22-24

CHAPTER 25

"Actions Speak Louder Than Words"

"That if thou shalt confess with thy mouth the Lord Jesus, and shalt believe in thine heart that God hath raised him from the dead, thou shalt be saved."

Romans 10:9

What is the greater measure of a man's character, the creed he professes, or the life he actually and consistently carries out? I've considered this question with many people, believers and non-believers alike, and the unanimous conclusion always is of course, the latter. What a person does is the greatest indicator of his or her integrity, of what he believes, of what lays undeniable, deep down inside the soul of the man. Two thousand years ago, James described it this way; "You can't draw fresh water from a salty spring". What we do in life is the reflection of who we are. James, like Jeremiah before him, understood that it's not what goes into your body that corrupts you or leads you to sin, rather man is corrupted by what comes from his heart. In matters of the soul, nature takes precedence over nurture, and inevitably, our hearts determine what we are made of, how we live out our lives, and how we are seen and remembered.

In the same way, Christ warned us that, "Whatever is in your heart determines what you will say." By this he wasn't naively assuming that men would always speak the honest truth. On the contrary, he was exposing the crucial connection between one's heart and one's conscience and the inevitable moral struggles, which arise. His humble advice was for men to reconcile their sin and to shed the burdens of a material world in order to see their way clear to unsullied decisions. He understood that when we harbor idols and grudges and unconfessed sin, the inner turmoil which results can often lead to the misrepresentation of self, intentional or not.

Bottom line, what is in our heart can be perfectly known only to ourselves and to God. So what others see or hear is a man's best interpretation, whether humble or selfish, of how he choses to exhibit himself in the world. Unfortunately, we can't always rely on a person to say what they really believe. Therefore, many people, if not defensively reciting what the world has fed them as the truth, are often just as likely to offer up a version of convenience rather than to actually bare their innermost selves to others, especially when pressed. The practical truth is that a man's actions always carry more weight than his words. In contemporary terms, words just won't hunt.

It should come as no great surprise then, that most people, cynics or not, will live by the unspoken rule that what they do in life is really all that matters. I trust my father is one of those men, but contrary to the morally relative fashion of our generation, I believe he arrived there from an opposite perspective. Rather than learning to be wary of hollow words like we sadly do today, my dad grew up trusting them implicitly. My father was raised in a time when a man's word was his promise and his handshake a guarantee. It was understood that those actions were not taken lightly, that they were founded in personal conviction that they were from the heart of a man. In his day, a man's word was inseparable from his walk. And so my father learned to lead by example, not by argument or ultimatum, he didn't have to explain his intentions, we just watched. For dad, it was more important to do than to say, words only complicated things.

In our youth, we were taught that all the excuses in the world could not change fact, and that failure to perform was rarely an accident, it was almost always a matter of decision. We learned that one's choices reflect the state of one's heart. We also learned that the state of one's heart was a matter of free will, that personal responsibility was a fundamental decision, that reputation was built from the inside out, one critical decision at a time, and that you better offer your words carefully, because they promised who you were. Just as James encouraged early Christians to live out their faith, I believe my father chose throughout his life to express his faith through his good deeds.

In light of his example I feel a real burden when considering the "qualifications" for salvation Paul described in his letter to the Romans above. While pairing belief in the heart with confession from the mouth Paul seems to establish a dual nature to the gift of salvation, a conditional connection from the internal man to the external man, from the faith to the act, from the private to the public. The worry is, that if read strictly by itself, this passage might leave an impression that salvation is contingent on both. But I'm not convinced that was Paul's intention. Is my salvation truly dependent on more than just my faith? It remains a difficult question for many believers and it does so for me, because of two persistent questions.

First, consider the presence of other references in scripture that appear to establish a more "narrow" interpretation, and second is the undeniable example of faith through acts that I have witnessed throughout my father's life. Admittedly, my real issue is that Dad no is longer capable of speaking on his own behalf. So how can I know for sure what I naturally assumed and trusted all along?

Can we extrapolate with faithful assurance whether a person is saved through the measure of their works, their fruit? Is it my place even to consider this question? There is no doubt that we all have struggled with this very issue in infinitely many ways. How do I know a man's heart? I believe in the inerrancy of the Bible, and I also trust in interpretation through context. Christ told his disciples when they asked how they could perform miracles, "This is the only work God wants from you; believe in the one he has sent." In essence he was stating that faith is the only significant action God seeks. Faith is a heart action, not a work. He advised his disciples to spend their energy seeking the eternal life that only the Son of Man can provide. Paul later wrote in Philippians,

"For God's way of making us right with himself depends on faith." In this passage I understand him to say that righteousness depends on faith, on the belief in one's heart. He considers no other requirement. While it could be argued that in actually writing these words, Paul is in effect stating them, nonetheless, his point is that one's faith, a heart action - and not one's works or words, which are from the heart actions, are essential to being made right with God.

Rather than attempting a theological argument though, which I am neither qualified for, nor educated adequately to attempt, my hope is to understand and articulate what I believe is to be one man's honest example, an example acquired through a lifetime of decisions made from the heart. For I have no doubt of the self-sacrifice, the uncompromising ethical and moral standards my dad has exhibited, the devotion to family, the forgiveness and steadfast concern for others, no matter the circumstances, that I was privileged to grow up with and witness to on a daily basis. I have no doubt as to the Christian faith that resides in my father's heart. The measure of his life has expressed it. He just has a hard time saying it. It's tough though, just sorting all this out while I try to record it, because there are so many voices, so many opinions all equally honest, all equally concerned that the truth not be missed. This is just my humble opinion and the ideas I considered in its development. It is not a question to be considered without the greatest respect.

Thankfully, I believe there are some fundamental tenets, which offer guidance. First, it is not the profession of our faith that saves us, but rather the possession of it. In the Gospel of John we are promised, "For God so loved the world, that He gave his only begotten Son, that whosoever believes in him should not perish, but have everlasting life." Salvation is receiving; not giving. God gave. We have only but to believe in order to receive. Paul tells us, "We were saved by grace, through faith, which is a gift of God." God gives us our faith, and through our daily walk we learn to trust it. This gift of faith in turn leads us to repent of our sins, believe that Jesus is who he claims to be, and also to submit to his lordship. Each of these three actions are heart actions, not works. All these three things occur in the heart as a result of the gift of faith and when they do, then we are in that moment saved, without saying a word or doing anything external. This moment of grace does not require a human witness and it is unique for each and every one of us who have experienced it. It is a moment, and for some a process, that can be difficult to define and even more so to explain, and so we are ultimately left to live it out in confidence and humility.

Secondly, it follows that the profession of our faith is the triumphant confession of our possession of it. I can't witness to what I don't possess. Thus, sanctification begins with salvation. Sanctification is giving, it comes from the heart, it is our works, our words and our fruit. Salvation is receiving, it goes to the heart, it is His work, His Word, and his seed. With salvation God promises an advocate, the Holy Spirit, which enables and guides our sanctification. Once indwelled with the Holy Spirit, Paul tells us we are obligated, eager, and unashamed to proclaim its great importance in our lives. It is not this confession or these actions, which save us though, rather, they are the eternally grateful expression of our confident hope, they are our works, and through God's plan they lead to the salvation of others. Jesus taught us, *"No one lights a lamp and then puts it under a basket. Instead, a lamp is placed on a stand, where it gives light to everyone in the house. In the same way, let your good deeds shine out for all to see, so that everyone will praise your heavenly Father."* It naturally follows that the lifelong expression of our salvation through faith is the earnest profession of that faith, and I believe this is the point Paul was making.

    We want to be secure in our own salvation, and in turn, we want to be secure in the salvation of those whom we love. It's a huge question, the question of faith. How do we know, how does anyone really know. How can a few spoken words have such enormous meaning? Can we ever truly be satisfied in knowing a man's heart, or in knowing our own heart?
    The answer, I believe, is the truth in trusting that God knows our heart, he knew it before we were born. He knows my heart, and I trust he knows my dad's. And that is my confident hope. After all, it is really only his omniscient knowledge and our faith that matter.

"For Christ has already accomplished the purpose for which the law was given. As a result, all who believe in him are made right with God."
Romans 10:4

CHAPTER 26

"Latch On To The Affirmative"

"The father instantly cried out, I do believe, but help me overcome my unbelief".
                              Mark 9:24

My life is blessed with a group of special friends whom I've known since junior high school, some even longer. We get together a few times each year for fellowship and a few precious hours where time sort of stands still and we can pause our busy lives for a day of celebration. Our reunions are a kind of thanksgiving, a proclamation to our brotherhood; to fatherhood and to the awesome gift of life that each of us has survived yet another year. It's inspirational to be reminded that even though time conspires against us all you're not so bad off as those other guys around you. But who's looking? Honestly though, its a humbling, joyful sort of day filled with stories of incredible success and triumph over difficulty that manage to find their way to the front of every conversation. It's been both a privilege and a challenge to be included in such a unique group. The kicker is that every year we have a Captain's Choice golf tournament and whether you are a low-handicapper or a once-a-year hacker everybody is going to see your game, so anxiety is peaking long before the day arrives.

The beauty of Captain's Choice though, is that every shot is really a new day, a new opportunity.

With Captain's Choice you don't play for an individual score, the strategy is not so much about self but about team. You can forget about the last shot, just step up and play this next one without reservation because the team always has your back. Captain's Choice is really not about loners or stoics, its for the man who is so comfortable in his own skin that he can open up without reserve, he can be all in. Admittedly, that's an awkward concept for most of us because as men we are programmed to be independent, self-sufficient and unmoved by any difficulty, which may come our way. Unfortunately we're reserved to a fault, so being fully committed to anything had better have an awesome return in store or we get defensive, we hold back.

Oddly enough, I've noticed over the years that the most successful teams don't always have the best players, at least not on paper. The teams that win usually have one or two guys that aren't so burdened by their past performance that they are able to step up without the weight of yesterday and smooth the shot of today. Its like being a pro when you're not one, or at least responding in such a way that only your best shot ever has a chance of showing up. It's like turning off the bad side, refusing it any airtime and releasing only the good. It really is amazing how every year the winning team has maybe one regular "golfer" and then a bunch of guys that show up without their clubs, or late, or shoeless and still they wind up winning. How can that possibly happen? How can you ignore past reality and excel today? And more importantly, how do you find success where only failure has existed before? The good news is that this is not a modern problem and the solution promises to radically change your life.

The apostle Mark depicted this dilemma in stark terms through his story of the desperate father. Scripture tells us that a large crowd of people had gathered around his disciples one day listening to them argue with a group of religious teachers when Jesus approached them. One of the men spoke up and said, "Teacher, I brought you my son so you could heal him. He is possessed by an evil spirit, that won't let him talk. So I asked your disciples to cast out the evil spirit, but they couldn't do it." Jesus was plainly exasperated and scolded the crowd for being faithless. He requested that the boy be brought to him and then asked, "How long has this been happening?" The father answered that his son had been possessed since he was a little boy, and begged Jesus to help him if he could. Jesus's response was abrupt and to the point, "What do you mean if I can? Anything is possible if a person believes". The father's immediate and miraculous reply was, "I do believe, but help me overcome my unbelief!"

Help me overcome my unbelief. Help me ignore my past. Help me forget myself and believe in Him. Help me disregard years of failure, false promises and downright hypocrisy. How often have you felt that way? You wanted to believe in something or someone, even your new self and you couldn't quite reach the critical threshold. You knew what you had to do and yet that extra special "something" that is required just wouldn't bubble up. It's like setting up for that shot in the golf tournament. You have to take yourself out of the equation. Forget about all the shanked, skulled, whiffed, chili-dipped disasters of the past. It's not about what I used to do; it's all about what I can. It is simply a matter of shutting out the "me" and letting in the Him. The pros call it "seeing the shot", planning what you're going to do, not what you might do. And as it turns out, the positive reinforcement is in the shot itself. It's the following through. It's the commitment. That's the realization Jesus saw in the desperate father, and once his faith was committed his future was assured.

We know what to do, but for a million little reasons, each of which, have their perfectly logical foundation, we allow the past to repeat itself. Rather than taking the bold measures necessary we often find ourselves drawn into complacence, even knowing that we face a bad outcome. The Bible tells us that this timid commitment, this cautious, maybe even selfish response to God's promises only serves to diminish or negate the true potential that he so lovingly planned. By thinking that we "know better", or by accepting mediocrity we are actually preventing God's vision for our lives. By holding back we are making ourselves more vulnerable to worldly sin, we discourage those around us through false pride and, unfortunately, we may even prevent the very miracles that God has planned in our lives. Doing the same thing over and over and expecting a different result is not a blueprint for success. Self-reliance is just that, reliance on self. Lonely self-reliance.

That's exactly where the desperate father was when Christ purposefully walked into his life, he had done all he knew to do, he had exhausted himself and he was all alone, which brings me back to the matter of my annual Captain's Choice golf tournament. The teams that invariably win with the greatest regularity are those comprised of players willing to discard the short-sighted, self-imposed barriers in their game, and if even for a day, rely on direction from without. They step beyond self. They succeed by freeing themselves of dead-end personal bias and placing their trust in a greater authority. By acknowledging that their own efforts will always fall short and that full potential is only available to those willing to accept it, consistent winners bridge the gap between failure and success.

That was the point Mark was driving at in his story of the desperate father. Mark showed us that despite his unlimited love for his son and unfailing efforts to seek help, even from Christ's disciples, who themselves were hobbled with doubt, the father finally and heroically articulated what we all have deeply felt in our hearts at some point. The desperate father had finally accepted his brokenness and in full appreciation of the moment pleaded for Christ to strengthen his faith, to help him overcome his unbelief. He felt it in his heart and mercifully he said it. God's word promises that's all we have to do. His grace will always, always take care of the rest.

"For it is believing in your heart that you are made right with God, and it is by confessing with your mouth that you are saved".
                                    Romans 10:9

Fathers Day Addendum:

As fathers there is absolutely nothing any one of us would not do for a child in need and the desperate father in the story above was no different. We read that he spent years in search of help to rid his child of this affliction, but without success. And if we look at this dilemma from his perspective it is difficult to see where the problem really lies, but when you consider what his son was observing it becomes crystal clear. What the desperate father's son saw was a dad who was honestly trying to seek help, but the help he sought was just that, help from someone else, help from another place, help from anywhere but his father.

In effect, the father was delegating his responsibility to a stranger to someone the child had no connection with whatsoever and therefore no trust. In a very real sense the child was seeing rejection and the unavoidable result was failure at every turn. It was not until the father humbly demonstrated his faith in Christ, and confidently invited him into their lives that the son was finally delivered from isolation. It was the father's willful, public, earnest profession of his faith that saved his son. It was this ultimate act of love that overcame the lifetime of rejection. It was the father living out his faith that in turn led his son to the One that would save him.

It's a subtle but critical point and James wrote about it when he said, "What good is it, dear brothers and sisters, if you say you have faith but don't show it by your actions?" That's the point Mark was making. Words are really just that, words. For faith to be real it must be seen in our actions, we must live it out, not in a casual or perfunctory manner, but really, honestly, humbly live it out. That is what the world around us, including most importantly our children, is looking for. They don't want to see us go through the motions, they are not persuaded by arguments, and they desperately want to see us live it out. It is only then that they will ever be finally led to faith themselves. The desperate father confessed it with his mouth, that is what we all heard, but when he finally believed it in his heart, that is what his desperate son saw. If you really want to see a miracle in your life, live it out and as Christ promised, "anything is possible".

CHAPTER 27

"Where Are My Blessings?"

"But if you remain in me and my words remain in you, you may ask for anything you want, and it will be granted".
John 15:7

    I have often wondered what God must be thinking when I come to him with requests which seem incredibly important to me at the time only later to discover they were either already provided for or not so necessary to begin with. It's almost unfair, he knows what will happen long before it ever comes about and in his great love, he has already provided for me by the time I realize my need. If I am fortunate, he has even separated my needs from my wants, making the eventual reality check that much less humiliating. You would think that after a while I would be comfortable and trusting in that relationship, but the material world has a way of bringing out the impatient in me. It's a daily struggle, the selfish clamor of our wants shoving past the humble reflection of our needs.
    It is an undeniable, relentless, ever-present weakness that characterizes us all, and not surprisingly it is a dominant theme in God's word. Jesus saw it in the people to whom he ministered and he saw it in his disciples. In fact, his first formal teachings, the Beatitudes, were his Father's promises to those who would faithfully

concentrate on their salvation, curb their material desires and live out the truth.

As children of God we are taught to value our spiritual needs over our material wants. So, how do we navigate this narrow path between what God has planned for us and the simple temptations our material selves so often give in to? How do I live my faith and deny my humanity, especially when my earthly circumstances can seem so overwhelming? The answer in straightforward terms - give as freely as you receive. In other words, live out my life as a reflection of the value my salvation imparts to me. But the skeptics among us would counter this advice by arguing that we really have nothing to give assuming everything we have comes from God in the first place and in that sense they would be correct.

However, what they would fail to appreciate is that what God is really, honestly, patiently after, is our faith, the freewill component of our souls that is unique to each one of us. The incredible beauty of man's freewill is that the capacity to live out one's faith is infinite, not bound to the material world, as it so often seems to be. It is this freedom of choice, which God lovingly waits for us to honor, honor not through material wealth, but through spiritual contentment.

In his inauguration speech of 1960, President John F. Kennedy delivered this famous challenge to people everywhere, "Ask not what your country can do for you, ask what you can do for your country." Those prophetic words undeniably evoke the crucial message from Christ written in John, as a universal call to action that those who are an integral part of a greater good should look to enhance and strengthen that good rather than draw from it. Kennedy went further to assert, "United there is little we cannot do in a host of cooperative adventures. Divided there is little we can do." This set the unambiguous bar, quit putting yourselves before your cause, that to do so would ultimately weaken or dishonor it. It was a solemn appraisal that man's purpose was no stronger than the men who are committed to it, warning us all it is one thing to claim membership, but quite another to participate in and advocate it. Without question, there should be no surprise that Kennedy's famous words still resonate so powerfully today, simply because they apply to more than just our material interests, they reflect perfectly our spiritual needs as well.

Isn't that exactly what God expects of us, to celebrate the miracle we live and conscientiously devote our lives to it, to walk it not just talk it. All too often though, we find ourselves slipping out of faith and into the distractions of daily life. This tendency to take salvation for granted and then to expect even greater is not so much a trait to be ashamed of, but rather a weakness for which to be prepared, and the best preparation is to be proactive in one's faith, to constantly and consistently ask what we can do for our Lord. In fact, isn't that what God's word is all about, if I will believe it and live it through my faith, my needs will always be met. Christ put it this way, *"If you *abide in me and my words abide in you, you will ask what you desire and it shall be done for you."*

The critical takeaway here is to understand that once we have fully vested our lives in God's word, the needs and wants which follow will necessarily be consistent with His plan, not ours. Under those circumstances no regret or disgruntlement should really remain as long as we are true to our faith. That is to say, if you live as the Lord directs you to live, you will want what the Lord wants, so you will be basically asking the Lord for things He wanted for you in the first place. Therefore, we are urged to commit our works to the Lord, and then happily our thoughts will be established. To have faith is to be all in, to embrace the good with the bad, to serve one and only one master.

So often though, our impatient self will read a phrase like, "ask what you desire and it shall be done for you", and like a laser we zero in on the words we want to hear and ignore or push past those we were intended to hear. So, rather than humbly conforming our desires to God's truth, pride tempts us into thinking we know best. Jesus warned us to "Take heed and beware of greed, for one's life does not consist of the abundance of things he possesses." He is saying, slow down, don't be caught up in the material world around you, it is a no-win gambit which inevitably leads us away from Christ and our true purpose in life. To be frank, putting my material wants before God's needs is self-righteous at the very least and worse, its a poor acknowledgment of the price Christ paid to buy my salvation. One of my favorite Bible teachers summed it up this way by reminding our class one night that no amount of wealth could ever reflect the infinite cost of our salvation.

So how do we arm ourselves against this inherent trait to want more than we need, to want other than what we need, or to look to the wrong authority for what we really need? Scripture tells us if you ask for things with selfish reasons, or ask for things that could damage your relationship with God, they will not be given to you. Make sure your motives are honorable before you even think about wanting to be blessed materially. Always thank God for what you have before you ask for what you don't. Never forget, if I make my faith contingent on God's gift today, then where does that leave me tomorrow when my needs may be even greater? And lastly, God said, "Try it! Put me to the test! I will open the windows of heaven for you. I will pour out a blessing so great you won't have enough room to take it in." That's really the key isn't it, forget what the world says and live for your faith.

"For God is the one who provides seed for the farmer and then bread to eat. In the same way, he will provide and increase your resources and then produce a great harvest of generosity in you".
2Cor 9:10

"So it is God who decides to show mercy, we can neither choose it or work for it."
Romans 9:16

CHAPTER 28

"The Greatest Among You"

"Well done, my good and faithful servant. You have been faithful in handling this small amount, so now I will give you many more responsibilities. Let's celebrate together!"
Matthew 25:23

George Bailey, an oft-thwarted would-be world traveler, who sacrificed his own personal dreams as the bighearted hero of Bedford Falls' Bailey Brothers Building and Loan, should forever stand out as an ideal example of the servant leader. Throughout the 1940's cinematic classic, "It's A Wonderful Life", George responds to the needs of others by foregoing his own, and in the dramatic final scene, the legacy he has so selflessly established redeems him at the critical, transformative moment. George, the servant leader, is saved through the generosity of all those to whom he has faithfully given, and shortly later, as the scene closes, the familiar nostalgic bars of Robert Burns' song "Auld Lang Syne" ring out, leaving us feeling triumphant and complete. George has his faith restored and Clarence has his wings. The past has been reaffirmed and the future promises nothing but glory.

> *"Should old acquaintance be forgot,*
> *And never brought to mind?*
> *We'll take a cup o' kindness yet,*
> *For auld lang syne."*

Auld Lang Syne is the perfect song to note George's heroic moment of redemption. It's a traditional Scots song sung to mark the end of one era and the beginning of another, to honor the past, yet with resolve, stride confidently into the future. Perhaps it registers with us so well, because we all inwardly long to accept our past, while outwardly trusting that our future won't be a repeat. It depicts that pivotal, introspective moment we must face when balancing the satisfaction and acceptance of one's material life on the one hand, with the faith and conviction of one's spiritual life on the other. In part we identify with George because our confident hope is to be there, to be vindicated in our faith on that final glorious day, but we can also harbor a little anxiety, because all too often we worry about having done enough. The struggle with accepting unqualified security is a universal human frailty so it's a tough question. Was I good enough that I can feel satisfied? Was my effort worthy of the fight?

Should old acquaintance be forgot so that I might confidently look forward with great expectation? From where does my permission come? Scripture tells us that Paul wore these very same shoes, and he took particular care to leave us with brotherly advice. In order to be a leader one must be willing to be led, in order to be led, one must be willing to serve, and in order to serve, one must be freed of their past. Auld lang syne, days long past, it never mattered that you were good enough.

Paul was certainly sensing his impending execution as he wrote from Rome during this, his final and most barbaric imprisonment. His second letter to Timothy was in effect his final words and they were both a defense of his faith as well as an outline of the fundamental work that Timothy would be entrusted with to continue. As the letter closes, Paul reflects on his life, "that has been poured out as an offering to God", and he makes one final humble summation, "I have fought the good fight, I have finished the race, and I have remained faithful, and now the prize awaits me."

What an awesome self-examination, and even more amazing, what a powerful faith he must have experienced in order to be able to reflect so honestly and without pride. Paul never once regretted his past because he could only see himself as Christ would, perfect and without blemish. He was, therefore, unconditionally confident in preparing for his just reward.

The unstudied reaction to this passage might be to label Paul as a boastful, manipulating sort of person who had a fanciful opinion of himself. But those who observe him more closely actually view Paul as a servant leader giving selflessly up until the very final moments of his life. Rather than the platitudes of a self-centered man, what we are really witnessing is the loving advice of a man who has humbly given his all and would only encourage those who follow to employ this same hard-won wisdom. As a slave to Jesus Christ and a servant to his fellow man, Paul is gathering all of his leadership potential into one final declaration with the hope that this encouragement will influence many others to come. So, what makes a servant a leader? How do the mild-mannered direct the strong-willed? Specifically, what is it about a selfless faith that resonates in a selfish world?

To begin with, servant leaders make themselves accessible, they are always standing by for duty. They do what's needed even when it's inconvenient. "You must turn from your selfish ways, take up your cross daily and follow me". George never went off to college, he stayed home for his honeymoon, and the wanderlust sounds of a train whistle or ocean liner foghorn never made his top-twenty. Like Paul, who committed every waking moment from the day of his salvation as an advocate for Christ, George was tireless and infinitely resourceful in preserving and growing the business his father had entrusted him with. He didn't ask for the tragedy that bound him to Bedford Falls, but he shouldered the responsibility and carried on.

Servant leaders also pay close attention to the needs of others. They are always on the lookout. "Don't look out only for your own interests, but take an interest in others, too". That anticipation only comes from the deep satisfaction of providing an active influence in the lives of others, be they friends or strangers. Real servants don't sit back and wait for an opportunity to arrive, they prepare for it, they seek it, and they seize it. George took the time to know his community well, including each and every person in it. He had his finger on the pulse and when an emergency arose he was already waiting with a kind word, a timely loan or even a pair of train tickets. Paul was no different. His encouraging letters throughout the New

Testament were direct and on point, no matter the problem, no matter the gravity. Paul lived his advice and his public, authentic application made it readily modeled by all who chose to follow it.

Servant leaders do their best with what they are given. They don't insist on ideal conditions or perfect timing, they take what they have, trust in God to have made them sufficient, and they soldier on. "May he equip you with all you need for doing his will". George took "mama dollar and papa dollar" and saved the family business. He set aside his personal plans for college and stayed home to resurrect a financial company with little or no formal education. Paul mended tents, he never doubted the authority of his God, and he trusted faithfully that "my power works best in weakness, for when I am weak, then I am strong".

Servant leaders treat every task with equal commitment, to assume otherwise is to place our wisdom ahead of God's, a strategy that never succeeds. "Whatever you do for the least of these my brothers and sisters, you do it for me". Whatever their task, servants do it with all their hearts. We cannot fathom God's design in our lives, we can only ask and obey. The servant leader leads by serving not by swerving. He won't dodge the task or ignore it as not being worth the effort; rather, he will be elated for any and every opportunity. No servant is greater than his master. George treated every loan as a big one and every client as his first, and when the bank was on the brink of failure George put his own security on the line in settling each and every account, large or small. Paul was the spiritual glue to the Gentile churches of his day, and he witnessed to Roman kings, but he was not above bringing his jailer to Christ. "Take nothing for your journey". He never took. He merely gave.

Servant leaders are faithful to their ministry. They fulfill their commitments and complete their tasks. "Faith is the confidence that what we hope for will actually happen, it gives us assurance about things we cannot see". They stay with the job until it is complete, always in the knowledge that completeness is an end-point known only to the Lord. The freedom of obedience is a peace, which exceeds anything we can understand. In spite of being beaten, George convinced Mr. Gower of his mistake. In spite of following both Harry and Clarence into the frigid water, George saved them both. And in spite of his uncle's honest mistake, George took the blame, discouragement and all, and led both he and his family out of harm's way. Three times Paul was beaten with rods and once he was stoned. He was shipwrecked three times and whipped "times without number". He was put in prison more often than any other believer and yet he wrote, "If I must boast, I would rather boast about the things that show how weak I am".

The servant leader is not an oxymoron, but rather an exception, that rare individual who senses his or her place in the world, expresses that reality through steady confidence, and, despite the ever present discouragements, challenges and their own human condition, completes the design that God has so lovingly and perfectly placed before them. Scripture promises us that, "he that is faithful in that which is least is also faithful in much". The servant leader is that special person who builds his or her reputation one small success at a time, doing so as though each and every challenge was the last. He or she does not have to look back with shame or regret, doesn't have to suffer the what if's, will never bargain for more time or look to blame others for their shortfalls.

    The servant leader is not afraid to fail because he knows he has already succeeded. The servant leader is "all in" all of the time. Like George, the servant leader prevails despite all odds because his work has never represented himself. It always represented God's greater cause. And like Paul, the servant leader knows "the prize is not just for me but for all who eagerly look forward to the day of the Lord's return". When you are a faithful servant to Christ, you become a natural leader to men. And the day you made the decision to become a faithful servant to Christ, the end of one era joyfully marked the beginning of another, Auld Lang Syne.

"You were called to freedom, brothers. Only do not use your freedom as an opportunity for the flesh, but through love serve one another."
Galatians 5:13

"No, dear brothers and sisters, I have not achieved it, but I focus on this one thing: Forgetting the past and looking forward to what lies ahead."
Philippians 3:13

CHAPTER 29

"Freedom In Obedience"

"And being found in appearance as a man, he humbled himself by becoming obedient to death - even death on a cross."
                                        Philippians 2:8

Freedom in obedience, that's an oxymoron for sure, suspicious advice at best, and yet, just audacious enough to be worthy of consideration. Frankly, this whole concept of obedience, even thinking about it, is enough to turn most of us off to any possibility that it could actually be good for us or enhance our lives. For the most part words like discipline, conformity and obedience carry negative connotations that remind us of painful times in our lives when we had to accept authority with no real reason or reward in sight, obedience for obedience sake. It always seemed the more we gave the more we had to give. The real struggle between personal freedom and societal conformity is for most of us a lifelong war, a give and take process that undergoes constant adjustment as we challenge and test the tenacious envelope of authority. This unrelenting, daily, dispassionate reminder that we are not the most unique, most brilliant, or most talented person that ever walked the planet, that we are in fact no better and no more "liberated" than anyone else is an ingrained and, for some, bitter argument against the absurd notion of freedom in obedience. That freedom and obedience could be conjoined in any positive manner whatsoever seems for most of us an absolute impossibility. But like all the other great influences in our lives, what at first seems intuitively impossible, often turns out to be abundantly true. This characteristic of truth despite worldly evidence to the contrary is an essential ingredient in the development and unquestionable validity that all foundational beliefs share. A rule that begs you to stop and think about it, to ponder it carefully and intently, now that is a rule with promise, a rule with potential life altering significance. The argument that we can become free, that we can achieve unfettered, unconditional, everlasting freedom through obedience is so important, in fact it was so critical, that God sacrificed his one and only Son as the first and greatest example. It was an obedient Christ who led the way and it is in his image that we seek confidently, to mold ourselves in life, all the while concentrating on the gift of everlasting freedom.

So, what constitutes obedience, how do we manage to achieve spiritual freedom through worldly endeavors? For starters, it helps to understand that obedience is a necessary prerequisite to our recognition that there is a God and that our lives proceed in mutual collaboration with God. It is not good enough just to believe, we must also acknowledge the sovereignty of God, his complete and unquestionable authority in our lives. Obedience then becomes the willful recognition of that relationship. One author explained it this way, "Obedience to God can be the very highest expression of independence. Just think of giving Him the one thing, the one gift, that He would never take." In this sense obedience is reciprocity, it is unconditionally giving back what one has received, it is faith in action. Obedience is proactive not reactive, it is willful, and it is born in love. It is a sign of strength not weakness, because it is freely given not taken, it springs from us rather than being coerced, it epitomizes self-determination, it is not an obstacle but rather the conduit to personal fulfillment. Obedience is the ultimate act of freewill. To obey in faith is to submit freely to the word that has been heard, because it's truth is guaranteed by God. We hear. We obey. We act. In this context, obedience becomes less about following specific rules and more about following the Word, and although obedience may be freeing in the sense that it allows us to become our true selves and to live the life God has planned for us, it doesn't mean it will be an easy freedom. Scripture tells us that,

"We know that we have come to know him if we keep his commands. Whoever says, 'I know him,' but does not do what he commands is a liar, and the truth is not in that person. But if anyone obeys his word, love for God is truly made complete in them. This is how we know we are in him: whoever claims to live in him must live as Jesus did."
1John 2:3-6

To be truly obedient, one must be fully aware of God's word and how it touches our own life and the lives of others. Obedience is to hear God's word and to act in love. There is no room for deafness. One must be able to hear the Truth and to acknowledge that Truth. It is through obedience that our minds are renewed so that we will have the mind of Christ and not our old, carnal thinking. While all of this may sound positive on the surface, there is no doubt that sometimes obedience can leave us uncomfortable or unhappy, or worse. Jesus taught us himself in the Garden of Gethsemane when he said, "Father, if you are willing, take this cup away from me; still, not my will but yours be done."

The opposite side of the equation is freedom. Freedom or freewill is essential to our progress and ability to become like that of our Father in Heaven and His Son, Jesus Christ. Freewill defines the quality and degree of our sanctification. Sometimes we have the impression that freedom is doing anything we want, but God says that true freedom comes from obedience and knowing what not to do. Part of our worldly experience consists of being enticed by both good and evil and then learning how to choose good over evil. How could we become like the Savior if we did not have the freedom to make those choices? By learning how to choose the right, we gradually begin to put on the divine nature, to pattern our lives after Christ's.

We find peace, happiness, and freedom as we make right choices. The cost of freewill though is our vulnerability to wrong choices, to worldly distractions, to the lies and enticements of Satan. The Father of All Lies readily avails himself of our reliance on the physical world for "reality" to lead us into sin. The resultant freedom without obedience is like energy that doesn't produce power, or worse, it leads to ruined lives. Real freedom is found in obedience, in subjecting ourselves to God's will rather than the will of the flesh or the will of the devil. Our carnal minds tend to think of obedience as limiting, but freedom is not restricted by obedience, it is released.

Obedience brings positive power, freedom, joy, peace, and hope. The ability to make choices is a crucial and wonderful gift, and we rejoice that we are here on earth able to choose good over evil and to progress toward exaltation. The key to finding freedom through obedience comes from the God-centered focus of this practice. If God is absent from the picture, obedience can quickly become a resentment-producing chore. But, when obedience grows out of a desire to love and serve God, we get a different and glorious result.

"Do not merely listen to the word, and so deceive yourselves. Do what it says. Anyone who listens to the word but does not do what it says is like someone who looks at his face in a mirror and, after looking at himself, goes away and immediately forgets what he looks like. But whoever looks intently into the perfect law that gives freedom, and continues in it, they will be blessed in what they do."
James 1:22-25

Man was programmed for worship. He can choose to be indentured to worldly idols and slowly but surely exchange his long-term freedom for short-term pleasures, or he can choose to hear the word of God, either way man must and will serve a greater authority. The bible tells us, "God blesses those who are poor and realize their need for him, for the Kingdom of Heaven is theirs." What could offer more freedom than Heaven? Obedience is not optional, but the degree of freedom is. Life as a Christian is not one of conformity to externally imposed rules, but, as the Apostle Paul explained, being "new creatures". We are to live and act out of transformed hearts. Jesus wants people to live from the inside out. To hear Jesus in this way is to offer one's self to be transfigured. To be obedient to the person of Jesus is to be transformed into what he is, gentle and humble in heart. "It is enough," Jesus says, "for the disciple to be like the teacher."

Freely chosen, obedience liberates us, and especially so for service since one is no longer the focus of our own concern. An astonishing freedom is offered for those who seek to hear Jesus in this way, but for all of us the process involves crucifixion. A life must be sacrificed. As Christians we are to live from our heart center, from the transformation represented by the Golden Rule, we must die from our worldly selves in order that we might live in Christ. Obedience is free from the guilt of going against the Lord. We have a clear conscience having followed by faith the teachings of Holy Scripture. His precepts are profound, but simple. His word is wonderful, but it works. His law is lofty, but loving. His decrees denounce sin, but give grace to overcome sin. His statutes are a high standard, but they point to salvation in Christ and they provide ongoing salvation from sin.

Obedience creates freedom found in the word of God. Freedom in Christ comes from obedience to Christ. The simple, glorious reason we are motivated to please God through obedience is that we have personally experienced His saving grace in Christ giving us a new nature with new desires. God calls us today to "come and see" the freedom, joy and blessing associated with obedience.

"Look, today I am giving you a choice between a blessing and a curse! You will be blessed if you obey the commands of the Lord your God that I am giving to you today. But you will be cursed if you reject the commands of the Lord your God and turn away from him and worship gods you have not known before."

Deuteronomy 11:26-28

CHAPTER 30

"I Never Knew You"

"Many will say to me on that day, Lord, Lord, did we not prophesy in your name and in your name drive out demons and in your name perform many miracles?' Then I will tell them plainly, 'I never knew you. Away from me you evil -doers."

Matthew 7:21-22

As members of the body of Christ we naturally assume that our works are appreciated for what they are, the considered, dedicated, determined creative output born of a desire to please God and to carry out his design for all men. A significant part of every prayer I offer is the humble plea that God provide wisdom and desire in revealing his plan for my life, that he lead me in the way which best serves my fellow man, be they Christian or otherwise. As we mature in Christ the voice of the Holy Spirit becomes more discernible and the wayward choices, which were once such prominent features of our consciousness are now pushed further and further from the immediate range of desirability. Unfortunately though, in complete comfort and sincerity, many Christians gradually find themselves doing God's work without fully appreciating or acknowledging the critical fundamental relationship that must exist between themselves and Christ. In a material world measured in terms of the actions and works our labors produce, it can be difficult to establish and maintain the correct relationship that God demands. We can become more focused on the doing and less on the knowing. So, imagine the surprise and horror of those people illustrated above in Matthew who had diligently, if not sacrificially, committed their salvation to the work they believed was a correct and sufficient reflection of their faith. Imagine having presented a lifetime of godly work only to be greeted by Christ as a stranger and unacceptable in every way. They didn't just lose their faith, or have it taken away. They never had it.

Is it possible to know all about Jesus and to walk in the light yet never know him, or more importantly never be known by him? The horrible truth is yes, and although James cautioned that a faith without works is dead and useless, the bigger problem is that works without faith is even worse. Works without faith is like trying to earn your way to Heaven, it cannot be done. For if keeping the law could make us right with God, then there was no need for Christ to die. So, in order for Christ to make the difference in our lives, we must know him so that he might know us. Faith, first and foremost, then works.

Early on the morning following the crucifixion Mary Magdalene came to Jesus' tomb and found it empty, as panic seized her she turned and saw a man standing nearby. It was Jesus, but she didn't recognize him. "Dear woman, why are you crying?" he asked her, "Who are you looking for?" She thought he was the gardener. "Sir", she said, "If you have taken him away, please tell me where you have put him, and I will go and get him." Jesus said, "Mary". In that single, miraculous moment she recognized him and was instantly comforted. Jesus knew her and he called her by name. She didn't have to donate a building or make a memorial offering or sign the guest registry, she just looked, she looked for Jesus and he was already waiting.

Don't we wish it could be that easy, that we would never have to suffer the uncertainty, the nagging doubt as to the authenticity of our Christian lives? That all we need do is look and be comforted. But the Bible tells us, "Blessed are those who believe without seeing." So we are asked to forgo a personal, in the flesh introduction with Christ and then encouraged to accept a relationship built on the foundation of faith. The tough part is that it is that faith, the object of that faith, and the strength of that faith that establishes the quality of our foundation. Faith must be built on solid rock if it is to survive the storms of life, which will beat down on it.

Perhaps the greatest and most insidious of those storms is doubt, not self-doubt, but the doubt that comes when fear seems stronger than faith, when we close our eyes and can't see the face of Jesus, when he is not where we expect him to be. Mary was in that place and Jesus knew it. He also knows it when we have stumbled there too. He promises, "My sheep listen to my voice, I know them, and they follow me, no one can snatch them away from me." That voice is the Holy Spirit and it is hearing that voice, being comforted in it and being directed by it that assures us of our right relationship with Christ. Paul wrote, "Examine yourselves to see if your faith is genuine. Test yourselves. Surely you know that Jesus Christ is among you, if not, you have failed the test of genuine faith." As Christians, we know his voice. The Holy Spirit is our advocate and teacher and reminds us everything Jesus has ever told us. The Holy Spirit is the direct gift of God through grace to his children. It is not given or received by accident.

Mary heard the voice of Jesus, she saw him as well, but only after he had revealed himself. Is that even possible today, could we actually witness Jesus? In a very real sense we can and we do. We do so through the way we live our lives and we see it in the hearts of those who behold the godliness of our walk. Jesus said, "When you did it for the least of these my brothers and sisters, you were doing it for me." What we see in the eyes of those we reach is not so much appreciation, or admiration, or longing, but trust - the trust of one who has witnessed Christ at work. It is the love we share for one another that proves to the world we are his disciples. It is the trust in those hearts that will leave you with no doubt that Christ knows you.

"You will keep in perfect peace those whose minds are steadfast because they trust in you."
Isaiah 26:3

*Nailed to the cabin wall of my bunkroom on the Ruth Bell River boat this verse from Isaiah was my daily companion, greeting me early each morning and watching over me every night. It is a verse from a song of praise to the Lord to be lifted up by the people of Judah. It defines the peace that God's people gain through complete trust, but I read in it just a little more. In a special sense this verse also describes the peace that those whom we treated received from us as servants of the Lord. We were given peace through Christ and in turn passed it on to the "least of us". Our patients came to know Christ through us and you could see it in everyone's heart.

About the Author

An avid sailor and lifelong journalist, the author is gratefully married to his beautiful wife of forty-two years. He busies himself as the ever-watchful father of three independent children, one of whom remains a skeptic. Through regular contributions to Bible study, discipleship, and life group leadership, the author has deepened his understanding and reliance on God's word, especially the humble responsibility of sharing and defending the faith. He serves as a deacon at Peace Free Will Baptist Church in Wilson, NC and participates regularly in mission work through World Medical Mission and the North Carolina Baptist Men medical/dental mission team.

www.ingramcontent.com/pod-product-compliance
Lightning Source LLC
Chambersburg PA
CBHW031441040426
42444CB00007B/923